THE WHOLE "STRAIGHT-UP!"

"I am from Miami. I am from the streets. That is where I learned to rap, beat-box and dance. That is where I learned about life, about prejudice and brotherhood, about hope and about hopelessness. I was in a gang, I have been shot at, I have seen people get messed up by drugs, I have seen friends die. I have been stabbed and nearly killed.

"I wrote this book from my heart. It's my way of putting the whole story in a way that no one could cut it, twist it, reword it or distort it."

VANILLA ICE

ICE BY ICE

VANILLA ICE

Plexus, London

Published by Plexus Publishing Ltd
26 Dafforne Road
London SW17 8TZ

British Library Cataloguing in Publication data

Vanilla Ice
   The Vanilla Ice story in his own words
   I. Title
   780.42

ISBN 0 85965 168 1

Published by arrangement with Avon Books, New York

I dedicate this book to my mother, Beth Mino, who I love more than anyone in the world.

Acknowledgments

I'd like to thank Randi Reisfeld for helping to jog my memory, explore my feelings and thoughts, and for getting my message down in a way that's completely straight up and true.

I'd also like to thank these behind-the-scenes people, without whom this book would not have been possible: Stacey Woolf, my literary agent, who fought for an authorized Vanilla Ice book and joined all the links together to make it happen; Bob Mecoy, my editor at Avon Books, for believing in this book and going to bat for it; Byron Mino, Tommy Quon, John Bush, Peter Seitz, and Gregg Harrison who *were* the links that, once joined, formed a book that I'm proud to call mine.

ICE
BY
ICE

INTRODUCTION

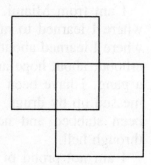

IT'S HARD TO believe that one little thing—in my case, words and a hook put to a beat—could change your life around so completely that nothing is ever the same again. But when "Ice Ice Baby" hit the record charts in the fall of 1990, that's exactly what happened. My life turned upside down and inside out. I went from rags to riches; I went from private person to public spectacle.

A lot of things were printed about me and attributed to me—some in my own record company biography, much more in newspapers and magazines all over the country. Some of what was printed was true, some of it was partly true—and some of it wasn't even close. Some of the confusion *was* caused by me; some of it was even *deliberate*. I had my reasons for misleading the media and I still do.

But a lot of what was written about me was put out there by people who prejudged me; who, without any real evidence, simply refused to believe my story: that someone who looks and sounds like I do could have grown up the way I did.

I wrote this book from my heart. It's my way of putting the whole story down in a way that no one could cut it, twist it, reword it or distort it.

I am from Miami. I am from the streets. That is where I learned to rap, beat-box and dance. That is where I learned about life: about prejudice and brotherhood, about hope and about hopelessness. I was in a gang, I have been shot at. I have seen people get messed up by drugs, I have seen friends die. I have been stabbed and nearly killed. I put my mother through hell.

I am not proud of my background. I wish it had never been exposed. But when I became a celebrity, all hope of that was gone forever.

My real name is Robert Matthew Van Winkle. Robby Van Winkle and Vanilla Ice are the same exact person, but at the same time they're two very different people. Robby Van Winkle was a terrible kid, but it's because of him that Vanilla Ice exists. And it's because of him that Vanilla Ice can be a positive role model now.

There's a message in this book. It's a message I'm sending out to every kid—black, white, Hispanic, Asian, whatever—with a dream. If you have a goal, go for it. Work *hard* for it and don't let yourself get sidetracked by anyone who says you'll never make it. If you have a dream, follow it.

Robby Van Winkle and Vanilla Ice *are* the American dream come true. And if I made it, so can you. Have faith in God and have faith in yourself. The bottom line is this: It's not where you're from, it's where you're at. It's not who you *were*, it's who you *are*. In this book, my book, *Ice By Ice*, I'm gonna tell you about all of it: where I'm really from, where I'm at, who I was, how I made it and who I am now. It's the real deal.

ICE FORMATIONS

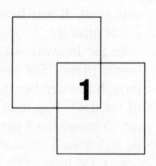

1

"If There Was A Problem,
Yo, I'll Solve It . . ."

SOME PEOPLE DON'T have a choice about the way their lives go. They really don't. They might think they do, but the way outside things push at them, push them in a certain direction, there's really no choice. You do what you have to do.

That's what it was like for me.

I was born in 1967 on Halloween. I lived with my mother and older half-brother Kip in Hialeah, a suburb of Miami. We had an apartment, it was a two-story deal in a lower middle class area. It was an apartment that we paid for, and not a "government subsidy" kind of thing.

We weren't in the projects, but we were a block away. I went to the same schools as kids from the projects—same parties, same everything. I hung out in the projects, more or less in the ghetto. There were these run-down playgrounds, but we didn't use them,

5

because there was always construction going on around them. Mostly we hung out in these open fields right outside our houses.

We had a two-room apartment with the longest hallway. There was one room for my mom, and my brother and I shared a room. It was tiny and cramped, but it was great. It was home, and I loved it. In some ways, I *still* miss it.

In the hallway we had this piano, 'cause my mom taught piano. She gave lessons to make money, even though I remember that the piano was out of tune most of the time. Kip didn't play. She tried for years to get me to learn, but I never took the time to sit down and do it. I wasn't interested at all. Now I wish I had been, 'cause I'd love to be able to jump on a piano and start playing.

Me and Kip slept side-by-side in a trundle bed, where one bed slides out from underneath the other. He's five years older than me—he was born on Christmas—and we were close in some ways, but *definitely* not in others.

We fought all the time, 24–7: 24 hours a day, 7 days a week. We fought seriously. I remember big fights, involving cuts and stitches and stuff like that. The worst fight we ever had was when I threw a telephone at him and hit him in the head. He had to have stitches. I did it in retaliation for him beating me up, which—now that I look back on it—I kind of deserved.

What happened was: I was looking under the sink in the bathroom, I don't even remember what for, some Windex or something. I never did find what I was looking for, but I did find something of Kip's—his underwear! So nasty little brother that I was, I ran into his room, waving them and yelling, "Look what I found! Your dirty underwear!"

All his friends were in the room at the time and Kip was mad—real mad. He yelled back at me, "Those aren't mine! Get them away from me! Those are *not* mine!"

He beat me up for it, pretty bad, in front of all his friends—big time. And he could get me 'cause he was a lot bigger than me—not just older, but also husky. I was this skinny little kid. Rarely would I ever beat him up. I would have to pick something up—like a telephone—and throw it at him. That's what I did that time.

We fought over so much stuff—toys, clothes, you name it—just any stupid little thing. I had these Hot Wheels, cars that little boys love, and Stretch Armstrong, a superhero doll with arms that stretch when you pull them. Even though they were my toys, Kip would fight me for them. If I couldn't throw something at him—like if my mom was around—I'd have to get back at him by attacking him when he was sleeping, which I did. All through my childhood, I got in a lot of fights, but nobody ever beat me—except Kip.

Of course it was a whole other story if someone else was comin' at me and Kip was around. Then he was my *slack*. Even though he whipped me—beat my butt—he would also take up for me if I ever got into any problems with kids bigger than me. That's what I mean when I say he was my slack.

As far as other relatives, I didn't have any that were real close by—not when I was little, anyway. My grandparents lived pretty far away in a small town in another state. We only visited them on holidays, like Christmas and New Year's.

I don't have too many clear memories about visiting

them 'way back, but I do remember that my grand-father used to make ink stamps. He did it at his house. And he made signs, magnetic signs. And then he also made little bitty things out of pecans and stuff. That was real cool.

I used to love Christmas, even though it was only me, my mother and brother in the early, early years. But we always had a tree—just like any other family—with a couple of presents underneath it. I never really believed in Santa Claus. I mean, I did when I was real small, but I found out early that there is no Santa Claus because my brother told me.

My mother would cook us a Christmas dinner. We'd spend the night before at home, and I'd try to go to sleep early on Christmas Eve. But I never could fall asleep, thinking about the presents I was going to get. I'd wake up real early the next morning and rush to open my presents. I remember getting train tracks and stuff like that a lot. I must've liked them when I was small. And my grandmother would sometimes send me a ten-dollar bill, which was great. I could do a lot with ten dollars back then—a whole lot.

The best Christmas present I ever got as a kid had to do with motorcycles, 'cause that's what I was into most by the time I was, like, six years old. One Christ-mas I was wishing for the baddest, the coolest, the toughest motorcycle uniform in the world. I wanted the whole outfit—from the boots to the pants to the leathers, the coat, the helmet, everything, all matching perfectly. When I got up Christmas morning and opened this huge package, I was so happy, 'cause I knew my mom had gotten me exactly what I wished for.

I also knew it was pretty expensive. That was a major big deal, because we didn't ever have any money. I couldn't really go out and buy presents for anyone, but my mom always found a way to get me what I wanted. She was always behind me in every way. And she found a way to get me that motorcycle outfit.

As much as I loved Christmas, it wasn't my favorite holiday. That would have to be Halloween, because I got to go trick-or-treating. I'd get really big treats 'cause it was my birthday. I'd go out with my friends, but we were smart enough to stay away from the projects on that night. Not only wasn't it safe, but there wasn't much good candy in the projects either. So we'd get someone to drive us to the nicer areas and get better stuff.

I really got into dressing up on Halloween. Every year I was something different. Sometimes I'd buy costumes, but I liked making them more. I think I just liked making myself up, putting blackout stuff on my teeth, fake blood all over. That fake blood was my favorite. I loved that stuff!

For the last four years I've dressed up as the same thing—a sniper. I put stripes all over my face, do a camouflage look—not like Army camouflage, more like an urban sniper. I like that costume 'cause it's simple and easy. I don't have to go out and buy anything, just throw some makeup on. Yep, yep, I *still* dress up for Halloween. Until I *die* I'm gonna dress up on my birthday every year.

Even as a little kid, I spent a lot of time in the streets. I was hardly home at all, didn't watch much TV. The only TV show I remember is Scooby Doo on Saturday morning cartoons. Mostly I was hanging out with my friends in the projects. I didn't do any organized kinds of sports—little league, soccer, stuff like that—just hoops in the streets, basketball. And played in the parks and stuff *all* the time. That was pretty much it for sports.

I was very inquisitive as a kid, always wanting to know what it felt like to do this, be in that—what it was like to be in fights. And yeah, I got into trouble because of it. I was the kind of kid—and this trips *everybody* out—who was never shy at all, in any situation. You couldn't embarrass me back then and you can't now. I'll do anything, especially on a dare. I was always a daredevil and that's how I still am.

And it's weird 'cause when I was younger, all my friends had fears, fear of the dark, fear of stuff like that. And I was never afraid of anything. Maybe it's because my brother beat me up so many times, but I just don't remember having any fears.

What I do remember real well is knowing that we were poor. I'd see other kids going to the movies, going to pro ball games, and knowing that I couldn't afford to do that. I was a big fan of all the Miami teams—the Hurricanes, the Dolphins. I would have loved to go to the games, but there was no way. Not only was there no money, but there was no one to take me.

I've said before that I don't have a father. And everyone says, "That's not possible, everyone has a father." Well, of course, there was someone who fathered me, but he was never any kind of father to me. The person who plants the seed isn't a father. It's the one who waters the plant and helps it grow. Up until the time I was eight, no one did that for me. But I didn't really resent not having a father. You can't miss what you never had. I didn't know what it was like to have one, so it really wasn't a big deal.

I wish I could leave it at that, but people don't let me. Somebody tried to play a joke on me recently.

Someone came up to one of my dancers and said he was my dad. It was some kind of sick, freaking joke, you know, something like that. But it didn't get to me. Things like that don't get to me because I really don't care about it. If somebody did come up to me and really *was* my father, he'd still be a stranger. I'd feel like, "Who are you? I don't care if you're my father or not, get away from me. You ain't nobody. Where were you when I was little, when I needed you? Nowhere." So it's no big deal to me.

My mother is the love of my life. Whatever I wanted to do, she was behind me. Even though I gave her a very tough time—especially when I got a little older— she was there for me. But she didn't have very much influence over me. Nobody had a whole lot of influence over me. I made me, basically. I didn't get anything from anybody. Nobody was really that close to me as a kid. That's why nobody can figure me out.

I always solved my own personal problems and stuff like that. I never needed to talk to anyone to solve my problems. I take care of them myself. A lot of people need someone to talk to, but I've never been able to open up and do that. Never could, never will. That's just the way I am. And that's just exactly where the "Ice, Ice, Baby" hook came from—"If there was a problem, yo, *I'll* solve it."

My problems—with school and with the law— hadn't even started yet.

SCHOOLDAZE

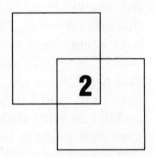

2

*"I walk the beat and I
walk it with clarity,
I wanna make sure
all is hearin' me"*

I'VE MOVED AROUND my whole entire life. We started when I was young. There were always reasons for the move, either better job opportunities, or just my mother trying to get me out of a certain neighborhood and away from bad influences.

When I was real young, we moved around the Miami area a lot—mostly around Hialeah and Miami Lakes—sometimes near enough to stay in the same school, sometimes not. We moved to different apartments, different towns, different cities, sometimes another state—anything to get me to straighten out.

I ended up going to about six or seven different elementary schools. Sometimes we lived close enough so I could walk, sometimes my mother drove me, other times I took the bus. One thing about all the schools

13

I went to: none were in rich neighborhoods or anything like that, and all of them were integrated. In a lot of them, black kids were the majority, and others were just real culturally and ethnically mixed. I *have* grown up with all types of kids, right from the start.

Because we moved around so much I was always the new kid in school. I'd always have to go through that and I *hated* it. I hated it a lot—having to start all over again, meet new friends, come in at half-year, walkin' in the classroom, *everybody* starin' at you. It's real rough for a kid. But I did it so much that I got used to it. And I found a way to cope with it.

After a while I started to figure, well, if everybody's eyes were going to be on me anyway, I'm gonna give 'em something good to look at. So that's how I first started dressing in a totally original way. I went through so many different styles—I always started my own thing. I would think of things that nobody else had ever done, and come into school on my first day like that. I wore cut-off pants to school before anybody else, or I'd come in wearing my pants inside out! I'd wear a boot on one foot and a tennis shoe on the other, wear blue jeans with one leg long, the other leg cut off, stuff like that. I did this before anybody else. I've always been 100 percent original. Now that stuff's the accepted style in a lot of places.

As soon as everybody knew who I was, I'd get into the class clown thing—make fun of the teachers, make fun of the work, anything I could think of. I always made everybody laugh, no doubt about that. That was one of the main things Robert Van Winkle was—a class clown, a real comedian.

The thing I found out after a while was that even though I hated bein' the new kid and *having* to make an impression right away, I liked being in the spotlight.

Deep inside, I wanted to be the center of everybody's attention. I wanted to be talked about by everybody. I wanted to stand out. I still do.

And as far as the kids in school went, it usually ended up that half of them liked me and half didn't. The half that liked me was usually the girls. All the girls loved me, and all the guys hated me because of that. I got into a lot of fights, even in elementary school, because of that. Too many fights.

Sometimes I got myself to the point where I just didn't care if people liked me or not. But everything went a lot smoother if I was popular. It was just a lot easier. But I didn't change in any way to make people like me more. I was just always myself, 100 percent original.

Since I moved around so much and was in so many different schools, I would always make friends, and they would become my good friends, until I would move again. So I got into the habit of never really having any long-lasting friendships. Even now I have a best friend, Darron, but I've only known him for four years. That's about the longest I've known anyone—except for my family.

From elementary school on, my grades were always terrible. It's not something I'm proud of, it's just the way it was. I was a smart kid, but never once applied myself to what was going on in the classroom. Half the time I wasn't even *in* the classroom! A lot of the teachers weren't too thrilled with me. I mean, I *could* do well, if I was interested in something. It's just most of the time I wasn't interested in their classes.

If I was even there, I'd be daydreaming constantly. I didn't pay attention to anything the teachers were saying. I daydreamed all day long. I lived for the moment the bell would ring so I could break out, go down the halls, yell down the halls, breakdance down the halls. Later on, I lived for the sock hops, pep rallies, stuff like that.

But as for what you're supposed to be learning in school, I wasn't into it at all. You'd think that at least in a class like creative writing I would have done well—after all, I write all my lyrics. And I always did like to write—but I'd write only what *I* wanted to write about. That's why even though I am talented in that area, my grades still weren't very good in English.

Back in school they would tell me to write poetry, but they would tell me *what* to write about and I didn't want to. I wanted to write poetry about the stuff that interested *me*. Later on, I'd want to put it in a rap. And their poetry, the kind they tried to teach me in school, and *rap* are not the same at all. It was always like "wherefore art thou" and stuff I couldn't relate to at all. I couldn't get into any of it. So what I did was write other rhymes in school, like dirty jokes instead. You can imagine how well *that* went over with the teachers!

Naturally, my grades were really horrible. But I didn't really care. I feel badly about it now, because I realize that school did teach me some good things. It taught me how to read, how to write, it improved my vocabulary—which ended up being real important in writing rap—and taught me how to get along with other people. Even with my crappy grades and lousy attitude, I wasn't the kind of kid that teachers had no hope for. Nobody thought I was a total loser or anything like that 'cause they all knew I was talented, very talented, as far as whatever *I* was into.

What I was into, starting from a real young age, was music. It wasn't the kind of thing I did in school— I was never in the school chorus or band, never in any school plays or anything like that. It was all on the outside. My life was lived completely independent of school.

There was always music in my house, so I was exposed to it real young. My mother was a music teacher, and she always listened to music. She still does. That probably helped me out a lot. I didn't listen to the radio. I got tapes and played them on my little stereo. I had this junior stereo–type thing and I wore it out. I had it for years 'til it just quit. I blew one speaker first, used it for two or three more years with only one working, then the other one blew on me.

The first stuff I started listening to were my brother's tapes. I think that a lot of younger brothers first get into whatever their older brothers and sisters have. For me, it started with James Brown. I was really into James Brown. It's not like he was any kind of big hero for me the way rock and even rap stars are for some kids—'cause I never did have any heroes in my whole entire life—but he was my favorite.

Right about when I started getting into James Brown, my brother and his friends started liking other things. Even though it didn't turn me on, I still heard a lot of it. Queen and the Steve Miller Band are what stand out most in my memory. I'd go through my brother's old albums. It seems to me that the way rap is now is the way rock was then—more danceable. Way back then, with the old rock 'n roll that I heard, you could almost put a hip-hop beat to it. It was more a "party jam."

Soon Kip's musical tastes and mine really got different. That was one of the reasons we really grew apart. He was starting to get more into rock 'n roll and I was getting into soul, and then funk. Being five years older, Kip just kind of missed the whole funk thing and the rap thing, too.

From James Brown I went into Parliament Funkadelic and other funky stuff. The first record I ever bought on my own was the soundtrack to the movie *Car Wash*. It was cool. I think I still have it somewhere.

Pretty much as soon as I got into music—which was real early, like by five or six—I got into dancing. It was the first thing I did—before singing, before rapping, beat-boxing, anything. Actually, when I started dancing, rap music wasn't even out yet.

I picked up the dance steps from what I saw the black kids doing in the streets. The streets of Miami— that was my dance school. I picked it up real well and real fast. Not that I didn't have to practice what I saw. I'd spend *hours* in front of the mirror in my room practicing and practicing those dance steps. First I'd just try to copy what I saw the other kids doing. Soon I'd start making up my own steps, adding my own twists to what they were doing. I'd mostly dance to my James Brown tapes and then to the funkier stuff I had. And I was gettin' pretty good at it, too.

As soon as I thought I was good enough, I'd go out and compete against the other kids on the street. We'd have these dance contests in front of whoever happened to be there.

I've always been a competitor. I feel like I've always had to compete against everybody. I don't know why, it's just the way I grew up. I want to be the best at everything I do, that's the way I am. Whether I was dancing, playing video games, riding a bike or a motorcycle, if there was someone else doing it too, I had to be better than him. I wanted to be the best—always. Why? I have no idea. I just want to be the best.

Soon after I began dancing, I added singing—well, lip syncing really. I'd lip sync to Elvis records, always in front of a mirror. You know in that movie *Risky Business*, that scene where Tom Cruise is pretending to be a rock star, singing into a hairbrush? Well, that was me. I was just like that, all the time. For me, *Risky Business*, that whole movie, was like a true story. I even got into stealing cars—and not just the family car—but that was later.

With all the music and dancing and stuff—and even with my mother teaching piano—I never learned to play an instrument, never took any lessons, never wanted to. In fact, the only lessons I took at all when I was a kid were karate lessons. But I didn't hang out long. Truth is, I only took them to say I did it. Never made it past the yellow belt. *Bought* me a black belt instead. Never became one though. Too much discipline, too much for me, anyway. I gave up on it.

As you might be able to see by now, I did not have a good attitude as a kid. It's not something I'm proud of at all, but it is the truth. Plain and simple, I was a bad kid. I mean, that's one of the reasons we moved around so much. My mother kept thinking that if she got me out of the environment I was in, maybe I'd change. But I didn't, not for a long time anyway.

I was moody, and had a bad temper. If I just woke up in rotten mood for some reason, or if some little thing pissed me off, then *watch out*. Nobody had better mess with me that day.

I was into a lot of bad stuff on the streets, even as a little kid. I just didn't want to listen to *anybody*. I wanted to do *what* I wanted, *when* I wanted—whatever it was—and not let anybody tell me I could or couldn't do something.

I wanted to go out and ride my motorcycle, go out

on the streets and dance, and do anything. I didn't want to go to school. And I didn't have a father to keep me in line or even steer me right.

I wish I could say I was some kind of completely clean-cut kid, but that wouldn't be true at all. I was a wild kid, and I put my mother through hell. She loved me a lot, she cared for me a lot, but she couldn't control me at all. She'd try to control me. She'd say, "Okay, you're grounded," or something like that. She couldn't spank me. If she did, I'd just run away or go crazy on her. So she'd say I'm grounded and I'd go to my room—let her *think* I accepted her punishment—but two seconds later I'd be out the window. I'd just do whatever I wanted to do. To me, it wasn't any big deal. I'd just push it to the extreme. Uh-huh, even 'way back then, that was my theme—to the extreme.

I put her through hell and there wasn't much she could really do. She *had* to work during the day, so I'd pretty much do whatever I wanted. I made up ways where I could satisfy her and tell her I was doing one thing, and then be out doing something else—go around her. Like if she absolutely forbade me to do something, I would pretend to agree and make her happy, but then I would go behind her back—sneak out, stay out late, leave school, and stuff like that. She used to take me to school. I'd get out of the car, but as soon as she drove away, I'd leave—pretend I was going in, but then just leave.

Partly I think it was because I just didn't have anybody to really tell me, you know, right from wrong—to really straighten me out like maybe I should have.

And, see, this is why I love my mother so much. No matter how bad I was, she was still behind me in whatever I did. And she did try to straighten me out.

I just wouldn't listen. You know, I was a very hard kid. I was very stupid—to be blunt. I was a stupid kid. I wasn't thinking right. Now, I apologize. I apologize to God about it, 'cause my mother is the love of my life, and I wish I had never done the stuff I did.

Like I said before, I'm not proud of any of it—but I'm not lying about any of it either. I'm not trying to prove I was tough, just to get accepted by a rap audience or anything like that. I *was* tough. And I did get into trouble—all the time. Keep reading, you'll find out!

The funny thing about always getting into trouble as a kid was my attitude about it. Although I really regret what it did to my mother, I was still always very positive. I didn't let getting into trouble ever bum me out. I was just this very determined kid. I *knew* that one day I was going to make something of myself. I think I knew way deep down that this trouble stuff didn't really mean nothin', that I'd get out of it one day and do something great. I used to tell my mother, "Don't worry, mom. Someday I'm going to make a million dollars and you'll never have to work again." Maybe she believed I'd make something of myself, and that's why she put up with me the way she did.

One time she sent me to a shrink to see if that would help. Didn't work at all. Shrinks try to figure out your problems. They try to understand people, that's all they do. And like I said before, I'm not the kind of person that talks to other people about my problems. So I went to this shrink and didn't open up at all. I only went one or two times and then I said, "I'm never going there again." And my mother said, "Oh, yes, you are." So I went and managed to get this shrink so mad—I sat there and wouldn't say one word. Finally my mother realized she was wasting her money, so she stopped trying to make me go.

When I was about eight, my mother got married to a man named Byron Mino. She was going to buy a car, and he was the manager of the car lot. I remember, 'cause I was with her and I even got to pick out the color of the car—white. White has always been my favorite color for cars.

I didn't get real emotional about their getting married. It wasn't like I suddenly felt, "Oh, wow, I'm going to have a father." It wasn't like that at all. In fact, back then, I didn't really care all that much whether they got married or not. It wasn't a big deal to me. Byron was cool. I liked him. But at the time, that was all. Now I love him a lot. But, at the time, the kind of kid I was—I just didn't care.

I remember going to their wedding. It wasn't a big wedding, but Byron comes from a big family, and they were all there. A lot of them are South American and don't speak English. I remember that making an impression on me. Not much else did.

Want to know the truth? During the wedding ceremony, I was sitting in the back with my Walkman on, jammin' out to some James Brown, or something like that. I wasn't upset that they were getting married, but I wasn't overjoyed either. I just didn't care all that much one way or the other.

But right from the start, Byron cared about me. And he tried, he really did. He never came on like he was trying to take the place of my father or anything—none of that authoritarian "I'm the boss now" kind of stuff. Byron tried to be my friend was all.

At first I didn't always let him, but after a while I began to appreciate him more. He was very religious and tried to teach us all—me, my brother and soon, our little sister, Alisha, the daughter of my mother and Byron—how God and family are really the most important things in life. That stuff didn't really sink in with me at the time, but it did lay the foundation for the way I feel now. And, partly, I owe that to Byron.

Our financial situation improved after their marriage. Byron always worked hard, always selling cars. That's his business. But even though the money situation got better, we still moved around a lot—I must've gone to four different junior high schools—because of better opportunities for Byron. One place that he worked for a long time was a huge dealership called Potamkin Chevrolet in Miami, right off the Palmetto Freeway. Byron helped me financially. He helped me get the things I wanted. And if I appreciated nothing else back then, at least I appreciated that much.

Sometimes he'd take me to a ballgame or play hacky-sac on the street with me. But since he worked six days a week, we didn't get to do that stuff too often.

After a couple of years—maybe three—my mother and Byron got divorced. Even though I think they still loved each other in a lot of ways, they couldn't live together. It wasn't a bad, nasty divorce—none of that stuff. They both loved all three of us and didn't want to hurt us. So they kept it very cool and just didn't live together anymore. But Byron kept helping out financially. After a while they got back together again, but never remarried. They don't live together, though they get along well now. They get along real great now, actually. And my little sister Alisha came out of their being married, so that was great. She's around 13 now and about the most popular thing at school—all of her friends go nuts over Vanilla Ice.

Even though Byron worked hard and my mother

worked, we still never had a lot of money. I wanted to buy stuff and go to the movies and sports games—there wasn't even any recreational program around for me to get into—but for the most part I couldn't. I'd see other people go to the movies, but I never could. It bothered me, but only sometimes when I let it. I ended up having to find other forms of entertainment. That's how I got into dance and rap music. It was a way to have fun without spending any money.

Everyone that knew me back then says they always knew I'd make it—be a star—'cause I had the talent, I loved the spotlight and I loved competition. I lived to compete—in dancing, later in rap, in racing cars, in anything. Everyone says they knew it was going to happen for me, that I was going to be famous.

And I knew it, too—only at that time I never thought I'd be famous as a *rap star*. To be a star is any kid's dream, and that's what it was for me—a dream, not a goal. But back then, the dancing, rapping and beat-boxing was just a hobby. My real goal, and what I was most talented in, was the sport of motocross. *That* was my career. That's where I was going to shine and be a real star. That's what everyone else thought way back then—and that's truly what I thought, too.

ICE CAPADES

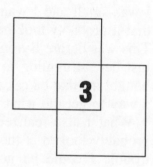

3

*"Over and over,
practice makes perfect"*

MOTORCYCLES HAVE BEEN my passion ever since I can remember. Even as a little kid, way before I was old enough to ride, I'd watch these cool guys whizzing down the street and wish I could get one and do that, too.

Lots of kids in my neighborhood had motorcycles. When my brother got one was when I really started wanting one badly. He'd let me sit and pretend I was driving his bike. I was really jealous when he'd go off with his friends and ride around, and I couldn't go. The big empty field outside my house was where he'd be, every day, riding around with his friends.

No one my age had a motorcycle, but, like most younger brothers, I wanted to be just like my big brother.

I started begging my mother for one. I wouldn't let up. I was serious, even though I was only six or maybe seven years old. At first she kept saying "No," thinking I was gonna get hurt and all. But she finally got me one. It wasn't even Christmas, and it wasn't my birthday or nothin'. It was sort of right before the summer.

I can't explain what that meant to me. Even though I was small and I wanted it badly, I also understood that it probably took her life savings to buy it for me. This was before Byron came into our lives and it was just her, struggling to raise two wild boys. But she bought me that bike 'cause, no matter what, she found a way to get me what I wanted.

What I also realized later on was that my mother probably looked at the bike as a way to head off any trouble I could be getting into. Even though other parents might've looked at it as something too dangerous for a kid my age—and I'm sure my mother was worried about me getting hurt—she also realized it was a real interest of mine. Truth is, it was really an obsession, one that stayed with me for a long time. But it *was* a focus for me. Maybe she figured if I was into it, I'd devote all my energy to it and not get into trouble. In one way, that was true.

It kept me out of a certain *kind* of trouble. To be in shape for motocross, I had to keep my body healthy, which was a prime reason I never got into drinking or drugs.

Like I said, if there was something I wanted, my mother would find a way to get it for me. I wasn't spoiled, but she was always behind me all the way. She's pretty incredible.

I'll never forget that first motorcycle. Over the years I've had dozens of motorcycles, but none of 'em was as special as that first one. It was called an "Indian" and it was about two feet tall. It had training wheels, but it was a *motor*cycle, not a tricycle. It was red and silver. As soon as I got it, I jumped right on and headed for that open field where my brother was. I'd ride all over and explore the neighborhood, go all around Hialeah. I started bein' friends with some older kids at that point, 'cause no one my age had a motorcycle—not yet, anyway.

I taught myself how to ride. I watched my brother and the others, but mostly I just practiced. If you do something all the time, you get better at it. Practice makes perfect. As I got older, I got even more into it—to the point where I'd skip school just to go and ride all day long. Soon, I was teaching myself jumps and wheelies and stuff like that. It was as much fun as I'd ever had. I really got into it big time.

What I loved most was the thrill—the thrill of jumping, going real fast, speeding along and just feeling free. I *love* speed, and I love moving ahead of everybody else, ahead of the pack. I live for fear and I love competition.

And I was good—not right away at six years old, of course. But over the next several years, I just kept improving my skills. Everyone that saw me back then said I was real talented as a motorcyclist. Everyone thought, ''That's gonna be his career, no matter what.'' They all said that, and I said it, too. It was my life. That's all there was to it.

Naturally, with feelings like those, it was inevitable that I'd get into motocross competition. Motocross is basically racing motorcycles on a dirt track. You don't just race for speed against other riders. There are obstacles you have to go over—hills, dips, jumps you have to make. It's like a steeplechase for motorcycles. You *do* go fast—too fast for the terrain you're on—but you don't really know how fast you're going, because they don't keep track of that. It's how smooth you go over the obstacles and who comes in first.

Motocross competitions are run by different tracks all over. Anybody can enter, as long as you pay the fee, which was about twenty dollars at the time. I got into competition on an amateur level when I was in around sixth grade. By then I had had five motorcycles since that first little red Indian.

There are different classes of competition, depending on how big your bike is, how old you are, and how much you weigh. I started off in the lowest level with a pretty small bike and worked my way up from there.

In the very beginning, even though I loved it, lived for it, I was still real scared—scared of crashing, getting killed—'cause you know you're gonna go wide open out there, racing against all these other people. I didn't really stop being scared for three years. I always get that feeling at the starting line, but, compared to the way I felt at the first race, I stopped getting crazy scared about a year later.

I didn't win my first race, but I did get a trophy. I got fourth place, which, for the first time out, is pretty good. And I was *seriously* hooked after that. Luckily, my family was behind me on motocross, because it became the thing I did every single weekend.

My brother was doing it too for a while. We'd throw the bikes in the back of a truck, get up at three, four in the morning—because the tracks and competitions are held all over the country—and hit the road. Everybody went: my mother, Byron, my little sister, and, of course, Kip and me. That's what we did every single Sunday. It's the main reason I didn't go to church on Sundays after Byron joined the family, 'cause we would have. But Sundays were for motocross, every week.

Pretty soon, I started taking first place in the class level I was in. It was almost a given that I'd win. I won first place about 300 times. Every so often, as I got older and rode bigger bikes, I'd go up to the next level and sort of start at the bottom of the ranks. I went from beginner, to novice, intermediate, expert and finally, pro.

The only thing I never rode was open class. I rode it a couple of times for fun, but I never did it to compete. I never weighed enough! At each level that I did ride in, I'd work my way up to winning in every single class of competition. I know that may sound arrogant, but it's true. And I got over 1000 trophies to prove it, enough to fill two rooms!

I'd race against people from all over 'cause, like I said, the tracks were all over—as far as Oklahoma, Virginia and Texas. The thing that people don't understand is why I never made any money if I won so often. Well, first of all, sometimes you only win trophies, and, second of all, it *cost* money to enter the competitions, to travel to them, to pay for a hotel and food for the weekends. Whatever money we did make went right back into the sport. It was really like a business—you make money, you put it back into it. Hell, I probably ended up *losing* money on motocross.

Of course, after I started winning, I got the bikes for free from sponsors, so that wasn't an expense. I rode for Honda. I've had a lot of bikes. When I got into it big time, I'd go through maybe fifteen bikes in one year. I was sponsored by Honda and they started giving me bikes. I had Hurricanes and Ninjas, dirt bikes, street bikes and motocross bikes. But there's gas and all sorts of other expenses. You don't do motocross to make money. You do it 'cause you love the sport—no other reason. And I did, with all my heart and soul.

I've been a daredevil my whole life, all the time I took risks. I live for fear. When I was doing motocross, I pushed it—100 percent. I gave it *all* I had. Yep, yep, to the extreme.

The biggest thrill of my life, up to that point, was winning the Grand National Championship for three years in a row, when I was 17, 18 and 19 years old. Now this isn't the competition that's sponsored by Honda, and it's not run by the American Motocross Association. But it is a *national* competition. That's why it's called the Grand Nationals. It's like the Super Bowl—you work your way up through the playoffs. It's not just the final race that determines the winner, it's the whole series.

You get points for each moto—you start with the first and keep going. After they're all over, the association tallys up the points to see who won. I won in the 125-cc pro category, both stock and modified, against 40 riders from all over the country.

The first year it was on a track called Swan, which was in Oklahoma, and the next two years, in the same class of competition, at Lake Whitney, which was in Texas. For those championships, I won not only trophies, but money too. 'Course that money, by that point, was going into my car!

Winning the GNC, all by itself—forget about the money—was a dream come true for me, just like having a seven million–selling record is now. It was all I wanted at the time, and to win for three years in a row was incredible.

I did motocross for over six years and during that

time there were some traumatic moments—really scary, horrible stuff that happened. The worst was when a friend of mine died during practice just before a race. He hit a tree and broke his neck. I was right behind him and I saw it all. This was on a track in Virginia. This kid, his name was Chris, had been on the racing circuit with me. He was 17. It was really bad. I saw them try to give him mouth-to-mouth resuscitation, and all that came up was blood. It was terrible. It was really stupid. I blame the track. They never should have had beginners, intermediates and experts practicing at the same time.

It hit me pretty hard, but I did race that day anyway. I had to go ahead and race that race—and I won it. It was like I did it for him. It was really weird, and I'll never forget it. And I'll never forget him.

I had some pretty bad scares myself, especially this one time when I got hurt really bad. I broke my leg, coccyx and both ankles at the same time. I started off at the gate with about 40 other riders. The object was to get to the first corner the fastest, and there's only one bike that can get there first. What happened was the track had been watered just before the race, and it was real slippery and muddy. Being the first one, I went flying. I slipped and flew off the bike. And everyone was behind me, comin' fast—at least 50 miles an hour—heading for that same corner, and heading for me. They flew through that corner and ran over my ankles. They happened to be going in a single line out there, so I got run over by *all* of them.

Both my ankles were shattered, but the left one was worse than the right. At first, I was kind of numb. I didn't even feel it. I really didn't know what happened. I actually tried to get back up on the bike and ride, but right when I shot up, the pain was so intense I just collapsed. It was the sharpest pain I ever felt, and there's no way to describe it.

Byron was there, and he came running out and rushed me to the hospital. It was a terrible, painful ride. When we got there, I still had my boots on, and they had to cut them off me. They took x-rays and saw that my left ankle was really shattered. They put me in a cast, which I was in for a long time. I couldn't even roll over in my bed for six weeks. I was in so much pain, screaming all night, getting no sleep, and taking pain killers which didn't help at all. I took the strongest pain medicine you could possibly take and *still* felt the pain. It was just that intense. To be honest with you, if I knew I had to go through that again, I'd rather die.

The hospital I was at was near the track. My doctor said that when I was under heavy medication I was hallucinating, going crazy and cursing real loud. The hospital couldn't wait to get rid of me.

After a few days, they transferred me to a hospital near home and I was there for six weeks. The worst pain had subsided, but only if I didn't move a muscle. If I so much as moved a pinky, the pain would shoot down through my body to my ankle. I couldn't roll over. I couldn't move my head. I'm serious, it was bad. I lost a lot of weight in those six weeks, too. I used to be bigger, more muscular.

The doctors started me on physical therapy—a lot of therapy. When I first started they told me—not that I'd never walk again, which I've seen printed—that there was an 80 percent chance I'd never walk normally again, without a limp.

The therapy mainly consisted of stretching, walking on the bad ankle, taking care of it—trying to get it back to normal. When you're in a cast for a long time and you don't use certain muscles, they start wasting away. So I worked on 'em for six months. During that time I couldn't race, so I sort of limped around on crutches, and made the best of it, went out with girls.

Luckily, the ankle came through fine. It's perfect now—I can't even tell the difference between the one that was shattered so badly and the other one. I can run, I can dance, I can do everything just the same.

You'd think after an experience like that I'd be too scared to race again, but that didn't exactly happen. All the time I was lyin' in bed, I thought about getting back on my bike, getting back on the track. I was ready to race again, ready to go. And I did go right back to it, but it was never the same.

Partly, every time I got on a bike, there was the fear in the back of my head that I'd get hurt again and the ankle would never work right. Also, by that time, I was starting to burn out on motocross. There wasn't that much of a challenge anymore. Now I know that sounds big-headed, like I knew I was going to win, so why bother? But it was true. It's like if you do the same thing all the time and you get the same result each time, it's no big surprise anymore, no big challenge. When the challenge was gone, so was I.

Up to that point, I was really concentrating on motocross being my career. I was doing that every weekend. During the week, just for fun, I was rapping, dancing and beat-boxing. Suddenly, when I got burnt out on motocross, the whole thing sort of flip-flopped and rap became much more than a hobby.

One thing racing did for me that ended up being real important in rap, it gave me self-confidence. In motocross, you can't doubt yourself. You have to squash that tiny little voice that asks, "Am I going to make this jump?" 'Cause if you don't, you could die.

So you have to *know* that you're gonna make it, you *have* to make it. Anyone that wants to rap—anyone who wants to make a dream come true—has to have that same self-confidence. You have to know that you *can* do it, and then you will do it better than anyone else.

ICE TEEN

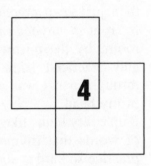

4

*"I live the life of my rhyme,
I think I'll let it show . . ."*

THE FIRST RAP song I ever heard was "Rapper's Delight" by the Sugar Hill Gang. It was on the streets before anyone ever played it on the radio. The kids in my neighborhood in Miami were doin' it, and pretty soon *everyone* was gettin' into it—singing it on the school bus, after school at football games, just everywhere.

Right from the start, I got hooked. I loved everything about rap—I loved the groove, the beat. It was smooth, it was slammin'! It was fun to listen to the words and learn 'em. I can still remember goin', "Hip hop, hippy hippy hop hop, don't stop . . ."

That was the first rap act ever. There were no other rap groups right at that time, at least none we knew of.

And, of course, as soon as we heard it and memorized it, a lot of us started making up our own raps.

35

That was part of the fun of the whole thing—seein'
if you could do it yourself. I saw that as a challenge,
and I took it.

I'd start thinking of rhymes, any words that rhymed.
At first, I'd have to write them down, there was no
way I could memorize them. So I'd write 'em and
then just keep practicing at home. Wouldn't do 'em
in front of anybody in the beginning, just me in my
room, by the mirror. And I practiced and practiced
and practiced some more until it started coming
through, and I was able to do them right off the top
of my head . . . "Say a rhyme, do it all the time, kick
it up every hour, like a nuclear shower." I'd just think
of words that rhymed and put 'em in a rap. If you
practice so hard at something, you know you're gonna
master it.

Of course, back in the early days, I did get dis-
couraged a lot. There were so many times I'd try to
force something to rhyme and it just wouldn't work.
Part of the problem back then was that I just didn't
have the vocabulary. I was only in seventh grade when
I started and, as you know, not a great student. But
as the years went by, I started to develop a vocabulary
of words that rhyme. Once you have that, you stow
them away in your head. 'Cause in rap, you have to
think ahead of yourself—you have to know what
you're going to say before you say it. It was hard when
I was younger, but I kept at it and sooner or later it
would come to me.

Pretty soon, I'd be makin' up rhymes anywhere I
was. Especially at school there'd be raps goin' through
my head. Because that's what I was thinking about all
the time, something to rhyme about. Walking down
the hall at school, I'd be thinking . . . "Walkin' down
the hall, kickin' up the lyrics hard, I'm rockin' through

the night, walkin' down the boulevard . . ." See what I mean? No matter *what* I was doing, it would lead to a rhyme, and a rhyme to a rap. Pretty soon, they were just comin' off the top of my head, without me even realizing I was doing it.

Naturally, I wasn't the only kid rapping. All the black kids I was hanging with were doing it too. Some people thought it was kind of weird to see a white kid doin' it, but a lot of people were trippin' out on a white guy rapping. But you can only trip out for so long. At first they'd go, "Wow!" But after seeing me for a year or two, their attitudes changed to, "Oh, yeah, no big deal, he can do that." So after a while, no one was amazed to see me rapping. I was just like any of my black friends rapping, no different.

This is when I got my name. Since I was the only white guy in my neighborhood doin' it, it was almost natural that they started calling me "Vanilla." So I became Vanilla M.C. Sometimes it was M.C. Vanilla.

I never rapped *with* a group. It was never like I was in a singing group. It was always just me. I was the leader of a group of friends, and we all hung out together and rapped. Sometimes the crowd I hung with would be my back-up, doing the "Yeah, Yeah"s. They listened to me. Whatever I'd want to do is what we'd all do, whether it was rapping, going out or whatever.

Pretty much as soon as I started rapping, I started competing in rapping. That's a *big* part of rap. Competition is what I live for—I was doin' it in motocross and now in rap. The rap competitions that we did weren't organized or anything like that—just a bunch of kids on a street corner, battling each other in rap. We'd always draw an audience.

I'd get up there, do my thing and then challenge the

next guy. And it wasn't only rapping. I'd compete on the street in rapping, dancing *and* beat-boxing. Beat-boxing is mimicking drum sounds with your mouth, and I was really good at it. I practiced that at home too, all the time. Thing is, I was good at all three, and not many people in my neighborhood could touch me in all three.

I rapped and beat-boxed at the same time, and I'd challenge the next person. "Okay, I busted a rhyme. Let's see if you can beat-box better than me?"

I was the king master rapper of the neighborhood. Not to say I never got beat. I got beat all the time, but nobody could do everything like I could. The good ones could rap real well. But when you'd go to beat-boxing, they couldn't even beat-box one lick. They'd be like, "Oh, I can't touch that!" And then when I'd go to *dancing*, they'd be really blown away. That's why I've said I never met anybody like me.

I've never met a person who could do all three things and be *good* at all of them—be the best at all of them. As for me, I'm a white guy who grew up in the streets. Not too many white kids that I knew grew up the way I did.

I learned from the streets and added my own talent. And I *practiced a lot*. I always wanted to be number one at whatever I did. Once I got into rap, beat-boxing and dancing, I practiced hard at being number one. Practice makes perfect, that's all I gotta say. And I practiced in all three categories.

People ask me if my talent is a gift from God. As much as I owe to God, I still think it has more to do with the way I grew up. It's what I got into, it's what I liked to do. It's just me, expressing myself musically.

Aside from being able to express myself in rap and getting off on the competition aspect of it all, I really loved being in the spotlight and getting the approval of the crowd. The crowd would surround you and decide the winner. You had to get them on your side with your raps. And you knew you did by their reaction, their applause. That was a big part of the attraction for me, getting the applause. I loved it!

After a few years, some other professional rappers came out, and I started listening to them: Whodini, Run-D.M.C., Roxanne, Howie T. and Kurtis Blow. Years later, there were white ones like the Beastie Boys and 3rd Bass. In fact, the first concert I ever went to was Run-D.M.C. I used to want to go to other rap concerts, but really couldn't afford to do it. I do remember that one though.

But even at this time, I still wasn't looking at this as a career or anything. It was still just a hobby. I was still going to make motocross my career. When I dreamed about being successful at rap, it was dreaming about coming up with something new to defeat others in the street corner battles. It was still just for fun, nothing more.

The street corners weren't the only place we battled. We'd go to people's houses, just show up at parties and start in. There were no deejays, no beats—just the challenge of "Okay, it's me against you. Let's see what you got."

One of my earliest raps that I used to battle other people was the one in "It's A Party," which is on my album, *To The Extreme:*

"Yo, I'm sparklin', like a towerin' inferno,
You wanna learn my songs, this ain't no journal.
It blemished my rhyme, because I'm drawin' the
    line,

> Don't celebrate too soon, 'cause I'm goin' for
> mine.
> Just a character in a made up cartoon,
> Like Witchel and Hazel, boy, you're pushin' a
> broom.
> So get a new life, or come equipped with the
> best,
> Mark another one for Ice, let the microphone
> rest.''

My earliest raps were pretty much about dissin' people—putting someone else down. If you're talking to another rapper, you have to dis' him. You gotta come up with a smooth rap. I mean, you don't *have* to dis' him. You can say other stuff that's not disrespectful. But basically, you want to entertain the crowd—whatever seems to be entertaining them is what you do.

Here's one I had that put a guy down in the romance department:

> ''I'm trippin' baby down, but you're dancin' to
> my beat,
> I'm a techno wizard, your boyfriend can't com-
> pete.
> Into your jealous bonehead, I'm knowin' who you
> are,
> I'm cruisin' in my Porsche, while you drive your
> Granny's car,
> Check the beat that I created, you know it's X-
> rated,
> Fresh chillin' style, 'cause Roxanne is outdated.
> Take my girl down to the beach, park my coupe
> in the street,
> Lean my seat back, so I can freak my freak.

No I don't like BMWs, I hate Mohawks,
No high style jeans, no fluffy pink socks.
'Cause I'm making up my own jam, my mouth is
   able,
To rock a fresh beat, without a turntable.''

Then I'd go into my beat-box. I got stuff to kill 'em on the beat-box.

Aside from dissin' other rappers, I rapped a lot about girls when I was younger. And yeah, a lot of the raps I did were *nasty*, dirty. But the thing is, I wouldn't do it unless some other rapper started cursing and dissin' me, and the crowd started liking it. 'Cause if the crowd starts liking the cursing part, that means to win you're gonna have to curse back at them. In other words, you can't just say a rhyme that doesn't have any cursing and expect to beat them. You have to come up with a dirty rhyme in their own category, especially when it's their crowd.

I could come up with some pretty nasty ones—there's a lot of four-letter words that rhyme. But even when I was doin' it, it never reflected how I really felt. It didn't have any meaning to me. It was really funny, just like satire. That's the way I looked at it. The words I said were bad, especially about women. But they were never the way I really felt about girls. It was just rap, something I made up to meet the challenge.

I'll tell you one thing. None of that old nasty stuff is anything I would put out today—on record or in concert. I don't need to put in dirty words to express myself.

We moved to Dallas more or less permanently because of a job opportunity for Byron to manage a big

Chevrolet dealership there. So we went.

Dallas was not what I expected—it was huge! And it's a *city*. People have some image of Dallas being like the TV show. They think it's cowboys and ranches and stuff. That's what I thought when I first came there from Miami. But, nope, it's a big city—which was good 'cause I like big cities. I could never live anywhere but. I gotta be around the buildings and stuff. That's my home, my tread, my turf. The traffic, the noise—I love it. I would go nuts in the country. What would I do? Milk a cow? I can't do stuff like that. I gotta have something to do all the time. I'm definite city people. And I always was, even as a teenager.

I'm sure that my mother was hoping that moving to Dallas would keep me out of trouble, you know, away from the old neighborhood, the old bad crowd. But it really didn't. I just found new crowds to hang with. I'd go to South Dallas and hang out on this street called Martin Luther King Boulevard. And I'd hang out on this street called Forest Lane. And I'd get into fights all the time. The street fights were getting worse. I'd come home with scars and cuts on me everywhere.

I did a lot of bad stuff out there. I got arrested out on Forest Lane a lot. Everybody who remembers Robby Van Winkle from Dallas knows I hung out on Forest Lane. Just ask any of the cops there. They'll say, "Oh, yeah. We know him real well." In fact, I heard that one of the radio stations was trying to get a street around Forest Lane and Marsh Lane, named for me.

What's really funny is that the last time I was in town, they all said how proud they were of me that I got off the streets, 'cause they know how I was. I was the kind of kid who *never* stayed home. I was always in the streets. And although I'm not proud of it, it's true. I was always looking for a fight, a challenge.

It's nothing to brag about, and I hate having to bring it all back up, but when I get accused of making all this up, it really ticks me off. You can go back to Texas, or Miami, and ask people. Go to Copple High School, 'cause those are the kids I had the most fights with. They'd come messin' with me and, well, I never was one to back down from a challenge of any kind. I never backed down from a fight no matter who the guy was comin' after me, what his reputation was or how big he was.

Hi Tec, who's one of my dancers, was one of the first people I met in Dallas. We were friends right off, and he can tell you that's true. In fact, Dallas is where I met almost all the guys in the Vanilla Ice posse.

I hung out in South Dallas, but the school I went to, R.L. Turner, was in North Dallas, or Carollton, which is more like suburbia. True to form, I wasn't much of a student. My grades were terrible. And I continued to be a terrible kid, pushing all the rules. I was always in the principal's office.

One of the things I did that got me into trouble was starting this group called "The Pep Busters." It was a bunch of guys, mainly three of us—me, Mark and Victor. There'd be other kids from time to time, but we were the main three. I was number one, Victor was number two and Mark was three. We'd go to the pep rallies and make fun of them. We'd bust 'em, go nuts—just do every crazy thing we could think of to disrupt them. Naturally, we got thrown out all the time.

We got a copy of the rules for school, which had things like you couldn't wear shorts—anything above the knee, that is. So what we'd do is really push it— come in to school wearing shorts that were just *to* the knees, knowing that it would irritate the teachers. They'd say, "You know you can't wear shorts." And we'd point and go, "No, no, these aren't shorts. They're not above the knee. They're right here *to* the knee." And I'd always carry the rule book, just to prove I was right. Other rules would say, you can't wear tank tops. So we'd wear shirts cut off that were *almost* tank tops, but not exactly. We'd turn our pants inside out—anything to make the teachers crazy.

We'd do anything to see how much we could get away with. Sometimes we'd come to school barefoot—make excuses like "Oh, we left our shoes home,"—just to see if they'd kick us out. And sometimes they did. They'd send us home, make us change our clothes. That was for a first offense. The second time we'd get suspension. I was always getting suspension, having to stay after school, go to study hall, stuff like that. Every day it never failed: The Pep Busters would be in some kind of trouble!

Another reason I got into trouble at school had to do with the way I looked—and the fact that other people sometimes didn't like it. I always had to look different from everybody else—don't know why, that's just me. So aside from wearing my clothes in crazy ways, I also started doing the lines in my hair way back then. And that was before you saw white guys doin' it. I'd see a black guy with maybe one itty bitty line on the side of his head. I figured, well, if he's gonna have one little line, watch *this*—I just did all kinds of lines in my hair.

Everybody tripped out at first and said, "He's weird." And that's how a lot of fights started. Everybody made fun of it, so I started kicking butt. That's how I got into some bad trouble. But that was in the beginning, 'cause soon after that everybody started doin' it. Then people would come up to me and say, "Hey, that's a cool haircut, man."

For the most part, though, in high school in Dallas I was pretty popular. That's where I really got popular, much more so than when I lived in Miami. Guys liked me in school in Dallas, and girls always liked me no matter where I was. I was still the class clown, my grades were still horrible and all that stuff, but I was very, very popular. After a while, even the teachers started liking me and even thought The Pep Busters were kind of funny.

But the kids in school had no idea what I was doing on the weekends—getting into trouble and getting arrested in South Dallas. They imagined me as a fairly okay kid. They just saw me being funny in school, making up raps going down the hallway, getting into some schoolboy trouble because of The Pep Busters. But they didn't know the real bad stuff.

That's why when Vanilla Ice got real big, hit number one, people from high school—people I barely knew!—came out of the woodwork and said, "Oh, yeah, we knew him real well, and he wasn't from the streets. He went to this upper-middle-class high school and drove an IROC-Z. He wasn't in gangs or anything like that." Huh! That's what they thought.

The gangs had nothing to do with school and people didn't know that. They just knew me as this kid who got all the girls. They didn't really know me at all. I moved around so much that no one, except my family, really knows me. And as you keep reading this book, you'll find out the truth about the gangs and all that stuff.

It's true, I did have a Camaro IROC-Z. I have always been into cars, into motorcycles, as you can see by now, into speed. I didn't have much money, but I

could get very good deals from Byron. I might not be
able to afford gas for the car, but I did have the car.

I had a thing—I still do—for white cars, white on
the outside, white on the inside. I swear I originated
the white car with the white wheels. It's called "white
out." I'd go buy spray paint and paint the whole car
with it, the wheels, even the black part of the tire,
everything. Of course it would always chip and I'd
have to redo it every week.

A white car is easier to keep clean. I had a black
car once and it was the hardest thing. I'd clean it and
go around the corner and there'd be dust all over it.
With a white car you can practically run it through
mud and it won't look dirty. Always looks clean. Even
now, I still got all-white cars—the 5.0, you know from
"Ice Ice Baby"—"Rollin' in my 5.0, with the ragtop
down so my hair can blow . . ." That's my real car,
one of 200 made like that.

So, yeah, cars were a big thing for me back then,
too. But like anything else—the motocross, the rap,
the dancing—I used the car to create a challenge, to
battle someone else. In the car, it was with drag racing.
I'd race anyone, even if he had a bigger, faster car.
It didn't matter. And I'd *never* admit to losing! If I
didn't come in first, I'd keep challenging the person
again and again until I finally won. I don't know why.
I just *had* to be number one, no matter what it was.

There *was* one thing I was definitely *not* number
one at, and that, of course, was school—grade-wise,
anyway. I skipped school a lot, a whole lot. I mean,
I liked to go because I was popular, but my grades
were terrible. I just didn't care about doing the work,
just looked forward to bein' with the girls and partying.
I would party in school, in the hallways, after school
and on the weekends, too. I didn't pay much attention

to the work. And basically, I was failing. When I look back on it I see how stupid that was—not to care, not to do the work—but you couldn't tell me anything then. I thought I knew it all.

Up to a certain point, I didn't even realize I was failing so badly. When I found out, that was when I dropped out. I should have been a junior, but I didn't have nearly enough credits. So I split.

Naturally, my mother and Byron weren't too pleased with this decision. I threw all kinds of fits, but they still tried to persuade me to go back, not to be a dropout. I kept telling them not to worry, that I was gonna be successful in life, and I didn't really need school and all that. But they knew better. I do, too, now. But like I said, you couldn't really talk sense to me then.

Finally, they gave up on forcing me to go back to high school. But Byron did insist that if I wasn't going to go to school, at least I should get a job. He'd say, "It's wonderful to have dreams of success, but you have to face reality too. You have to make a living now." I didn't argue with him.

So he got me a job working at his car lot. I did stuff like lining up the new cars. I didn't really mind. I *did* goof off a lot, going home for these long lunches, not coming back sometimes. The main thing was that I was making some money—money that went right back into my car, for gas and stereo systems and stuff. But I did work. I also built stereo systems for other people during that time. In fact, I was working on the car lot even after I had a record deal! But that comes later . . .

One of the promises I made to my mother and to Byron when I dropped out was that somehow I *would* take care of finishing my education. And a part of me really did want to. See, my brother Kip dropped out, and there was something in me that didn't want to be like that. Just wanted to be, you know, the first one in my family to have that diploma, besides my mother, of course. So while I was working I enrolled in a correspondence course. It was called The American School and it was all through the mail. I took the courses and did finally graduate that way.

I really didn't know how important high school was when I was in it, how important it really was to do the work and all. And see, the thing is, if I hadn't been successful as Vanilla Ice, I'd have really been in trouble. Without proper schooling, I probably wouldn't have been able to get any kind of a job, except maybe in a parking lot or something. Luck played a big part in my life, but you can't count on luck.

I know that the way I did it, dropping out and going to correspondence school, doesn't make me a great role model. You really do need to finish school. You shouldn't mess around as much as I did. When I had to get my diploma through The American School, working alone, I learned a lot. I also figured out that it would have been easier and more fun to do it in school.

I can only hope that if any kids are looking up to me, they see me and listen to me the way I am *now*, and understand that I am not proud of the kind of teenager I was. In fact, I'm ashamed. And it took a lot to get me to change and open my eyes. It took almost getting killed.

ON THIN ICE

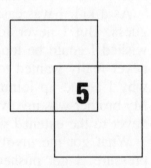

5

*"...Slice like a ninja,
cut like a razor blade,
so fast..."*

IN MY NEIGHBORHOOD in Miami and in some parts of Dallas where I hung out, there were always gangs. It was just a part of life as I knew it. Even when I was a small kid, I was aware of them. My brother would tell me about them, and I would see them in the streets—hanging out together, looking tough.

At first I was scared of them like everybody else. There were all kinds of gangs. Some went around beating people up for no reason, those were the small-time, nothing gangs. We had gangs that did stuff strictly with drugs—actually, they made money, like a professional gang. Then there were gangs that stole cars and robbed houses and stuff like that.

There were gangs of different nationalities. There were black gangs, white gangs, Cuban and Puerto

Rican gangs. Some were mixed racially, but never equally mixed. There'd be mostly white gangs with a couple of blacks in them, and in the black gangs every once in a while there'd be a few whites. I'm not going to say the names of any particular gangs I knew, 'cause that would be a mistake—a big mistake.

As a kid, I was easily influenced like most kids, I guess. But I never looked up to the gangs—never wished I could be tough like them, be part of them, never really wanted to be part of them. That wasn't why I ended up joining one, which I did, big time. My brother was involved a little, but only briefly, and never to the extent I was.

What got me involved was pure and simple peer pressure. I got pushed into it. Maybe I could have resisted, but I didn't. When I got to be a teenager, even starting at 13 and 14, it seemed that all my friends were into them. And this is the way it seemed to me at the time: either join my friends or have no friends.

Not only that, but they seemed to be having so much fun running with the gangs. I'd keep hearing stories and stuff. Like, they'd say, "Man, we took this car out last night and we had a blast. We went out and took it in the field, did doughnuts in it. Ran it into a ditch, crashed it against a wall, just had a blast man, it was fun. Had the stereo cranked up all the way. Oh, man, it was great." And *everybody* was talkin' this way. I was like, "Oh, *man*, that sounds like fun."

There were some kids who didn't join the gangs. They were looked at as "mama's boys." Everybody would taunt them and call them names. They were nothing at school, they weren't anything on the streets, they were just nobodies. I could never stand to be a nobody.

Some of the kids that didn't join also got beat up.

I'd see that happening a lot. So it was a combination of things that led me to join—I didn't want to be left out of the fun and I sure as hell didn't want to get beat up either.

My first gang was pretty much made up of all my friends. The majority of kids in it were black, and there were two Cubans. Some older kids had started it, and they led us into it. Soon we took over.

Some of the gangs in my neighborhood had a cause, really stood for something, had some point to make—not ours. Ours was not a big-time gang in that way. We were mainly out to have a good time. What we were doin' was bad stuff, but we were just out to have a good time doing it.

We started off cruising around on skateboards. This was before we could drive. We'd hang out in alleyways, and wander the neighborhood, spray painting graffiti all over. We'd spray paint the name of our gang on any wall or surface we could find. At first the older kids in the gang showed us how. Then we took over and did it ourselves. We also went around with the older kids and tried to pick up girls. I'd tell people I was older than I really was, even though I didn't look it at all!

We never got caught. Then we got into other things, which I will describe. But right off I want to say that we were never into drugs—as a gang anyway. I never did drugs of any kind. We didn't smoke and we didn't drink either. For me, I really had to keep clean for motocross, so at least that kept me away from the self-destructive stuff. I'll admit that some people in our gang did get into drugs, but those guys always quit the gang 'cause they didn't have time for us anymore.

We also never mugged anybody—at least anybody that wasn't in a rival gang—which isn't to say that we didn't go looking for trouble, looking for fights, 'cause we did.

We'd go to the mall and stuff, and if anybody messed with us, we wouldn't take *anything* from *any-body*. We dressed the way we wanted to dress, we did our hair the way we wanted. If anybody criticized us or made fun of us, we started a fight. If you saw a picture of me back then you probably wouldn't recognize me, 'cause I looked completely different from the way I look now. At times my hair was real short and at others, real long, with like a two-foot long rattail. I even had an Afro at one time. People really trip out on that! Got a picture of it, but I'd never let that one out! Didn't have lines in my hair the way I do now.

If you've ever been in a gang, you know there is no such thing as a fair fight. That makes me laugh—fair fight, huh! That's the way they portray gangs on TV, but that isn't the way gangs are at all. If someone took on one of us, he took on all of us. If the rest of my group was with me, or if even one friend was with me, we'd all be kicking this dude's butt. It didn't even matter if the dude was a wimp and I could whip him all by myself—the rest of the gang got in with it and started beating him up. It's all part of real gang fights.

We had something we called the "bum rush." That was when one guy was fighting another, one-on-one, and then suddenly another guy would come up from behind and knock one of the guys completely out. Boom! *That* was fair back in my neighborhood.

Aside from always being in fights, other things we did back then—and I am definitely not proud of this, but I feel I have to explain it—was steal cars, just to go out and have a good time with them. Wrecked a couple of cars on telephone poles—that's how I learned to drive! I even stole my mother's car, crashed it right in front of the house, too. I was turning a corner too sharp and crashed into a telephone pole—totally messed up the back and the side door.

Naturally, she found out about it. I just told her a lie—that I was backing the car out to get my motorcycle from the garage and didn't want to wake her up to do it. She didn't believe me and tried to ground me, but that didn't do much good.

Did I know this stuff was wrong? Sure. And in the beginning, I was scared and didn't really want to do it. But, like with joining the gang in the first place, it was peer pressure that made me continue. Truth is, it *was* fun. We'd get away with it the first time, then the second, third and fourth times—and by then I wasn't scared anymore. And by then, it was no big deal to me to go out and do these things. Didn't even think about it being wrong anymore.

My mother tried all sorts of things to straighten me out—especially when I was stealing cars, when I was getting real bad in the street. Once, she put me in what I'd call a "correctional facility." It wasn't exactly a juvenile home. It was more for kids with personal problems, emotional problems, not really for kids like me who were just plain messing up. I really didn't belong there. I belonged in a place for kids who *were* messing up, 'cause that's what I was doing, but my mother didn't want to put me in with other bad kids. She thought I'd mix with them and then get even worse ideas.

A bus picked me up every day and, instead of going to school, I'd go there. The counsellors there tried to educate me, get me to go with God, tried to get me to talk about my problems. It didn't work at all. My main problem at the time was that I hated it there—

they made me cut my hair!—and tried everything I could to get out. Between that and schoolwork, it was just too much. So I did everything I could to get them to kick me out. And, finally, after a couple of months, they did. They just told my mother that this was a place for kids with problems—not for kid gangsters. They suggested she send me to another place, one that really disciplines tough kids, but she didn't. That wouldn't have worked anyway. I just would have rebelled against that one too, and probably would have gotten worse.

I was just a terrible kid, a bad kid. I am definitely not proud of the way I was and still feel bad about it, feel ashamed. I was just plain stupid as a kid, wasn't using my brain at all. I put my mother through hell, and that's the worst part of it all. Half the kids in my gang are probably in prison now, or maybe dead. I might have been, too, until one major incident changed my life for good. That was the night I got stabbed.

It happened one night, right between Christmas and New Year's, on a street corner in Richardson, Texas. That's the kind of neighborhood where you wouldn't expect those things to happen, 'cause it's in North Dallas and you don't hear about stabbings in that part of town. But the truth is, I was there for a reason: My friends and I went there looking for a fight, and, man, we got one.

The whole thing started out of retaliation. A bunch of guys from another gang beat up a friend of mine at the Prestonwood Mall. So about a week later, I got it in my head to get revenge for my friend—'cause, like I said, when you take on one of us, you take on all of us. So about two o'clock in the morning, me and two friends went looking for this guy who beat up my friend. We actually went to his house, 'cause we knew where he lived.

We were going to throw a brick through his window, just go mess with him. We'd been planning this. But somebody told him we were coming, and he was waiting for us. When we got out of our car, he was standing there. Right away we started fighting him. There were three of us and only one of him. I didn't know he had a knife.

At one point during the fight, he came up behind me and I put him in a headlock. But he had one hand free and with the knife—it was a butterfly knife—started stabbing me down the side of my leg and my back. While I was trying to grab the knife away from him, he stabbed me in my hand, too. Altogether, he stabbed me five times.

I didn't even *know* it when he was doing it! I thought he was just hitting me real hard, 'cause that's what it felt like. It was night, it was dark. After a few seconds of fighting with him, I was totally out of breath—it was almost like running a marathon. I let go of him and moved away. I bent over slightly, tried to put my hands on my knees and catch my breath, when my hands slipped right off my legs. My clothes were ripped and blood was gushing out from everywhere. He got an artery right in my leg. That's when I realized that my hand and everything was sliced open. There was blood everywhere.

My leg was numb, and I started limping towards the car. My friends grabbed me and took me to the car. Soon there was blood all over the hood of the car from me trying to hold myself up, leaning on it. All I remember thinking was, "Oh, no, I'm not even 19 years old and I'm gonna die . . ." My friends put me in the passenger seat and took me to the hospital. Halfway there, I passed out.

When I got to the hospital, they had to cut off all my clothes, they were soaked with blood. When my mother got there, the first thing she saw was my blood-soaked pants and *she* passed out! They had to revive her! When they worked on me, they couldn't even tell exactly where the wounds were at first, that's how much blood there was. During a lot of this time, I was pretty much unconscious—but I'll never forget the sharp pain I felt when I came to for the first time. I woke up for maybe 30 seconds and the pain was so bad I just passed back out again.

What they did was put this thing that looked like a giant Q-tip with alcohol on it down inside my leg to plug up the artery. I didn't know it then, but I found out later that I'd lost half the blood in my body. You only have eight pints, and I'd already lost four. For a long time, I was just floating in and out of consciousness. Every time I woke up, the pain was so bad, I'd be screaming like mad. I'd never felt so much pain in my life, except maybe for the motorcycle accident. And my mother was there, crying hysterically, and going nuts.

The wound in my leg was the worst. He'd stabbed me in the back of the leg, but it was deep and went sideways and got my butt, too. Blood was just spurting everywhere and they were working like crazy to stop the flow.

Whenever I would wake up, it would hurt like crazy. I couldn't move without my whole body hurting. I was in the hospital for a month, during which time they'd pull the bandages on and off, trying to seal up the artery and keep it from getting infected. I had to have transfusions and surgery. They put metal staples in my leg and about 60 stitches in my hand.

When I finally woke up and stayed up for a while, I was in a hospital bed, all wrapped up and everything. I remember looking out the window and the sun was up. I just looked out and thought, "Whoa, I'm *alive*." I really thought, whenever I'd been conscious, anyway, that I wasn't going to come out of this one. I really thought I was going to die. Out loud I said— and I really meant it—"I'm alive. Thank God." I mean, *seriously*, "Thank God."

And that's when I realized I had to change. I said to myself, "I'm chillin' out man, I almost lost my life." 'Cause I never thought something like that would ever happen to me. Up to that point I only heard about other people getting killed, *never* thought it could happen to me.

And I just automatically, you know, said, "There's no way I'm going to do that stuff again. I'm not going to fight anymore. I'm not messin' with that stuff anymore." Some of the gang members tried to visit me in the hospital to see if I was all right, but I wouldn't see them. I decided there and then to just stop associating with them. I knew that was the only way to get out of it.

You can't even talk to any of them, not even once, 'cause you'll be drawn right back into it. You've got to be yourself and mind yourself. You've got to get one friend who's not in a gang and stick with him. Don't worry about what everyone else thinks. From that moment on, that's what I did. I just played it real low-key after that.

At the same time, I started to think more about God and what He had done for me. And I started praying, saying, "Thank you, God. Thank you for letting me live.'' Because I knew that He could have taken my life right then, just like that, no ifs, ands or buts. He could've just taken me. But I guess it wasn't my time. I *know* that God saved my life. It's the only thing that saved me.

I can't keep saying it enough—I'm writing all this stuff because it's true, it happened, and so many people are calling me a liar. I wish I didn't have to talk about it. I wish it had never happened, but it did. And people don't believe it. So I'm writing about it, but I'm not proud of it. I'm not proud of my life. I'm not proud of getting stabbed. I almost died. That's nothing to be proud of. I'm ashamed that I hurt people. I'm not proud that I stole cars, or beat people up. I'm not proud of the life I had before. And I do not think that my life is any kind of role model for any kid.

I cannot change the past. But God can change your future. And that's what happened to me. He gave me a second chance. I lived and I said, ''Hey, man, if I don't straighten up now, I'm either going to end up in jail or dead real soon.'' So I made my decision. With God guiding me, I got out of the streets and completely turned my life around. I'll never forget where I came from—and I have no reason to lie about that—but I'll never go back to the streets again, no matter what.

I'm with God now. God is the one that got me here and gave me a second chance to live. I don't believe in any one organized religion. There's too many of them to believe in a certain one. But I believe in God, 100 percent.

THE ICEMAN COMETH

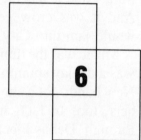

6

*"Roller with the rhythm,
I did it 4 my opponent,
If there was a crown 2B taken,
yea, I would own it."*

WHEN I FIRST came to Dallas, I started asking around about where's a cool place to go to hear some good hip-hop music. I knew there were a lot of clubs around, I just didn't know the good ones. Two names kept coming up: Monopoly's Park Place, which was more of a soul music club, and City Lights, which started out being a soul club, but by the time I got there was mostly hip-hop. Both clubs were open from Thursdays to Sundays, and definitely catered to a late-night crowd, staying open 'til four or five in the morning.

Both clubs were real tough, but City Lights, being in South Dallas, was the rougher one. When fights broke out, they'd be more than just fist fights. Some of those guys carried guns. But there were fights breaking out at both clubs, inside and out. I was around it all.

City Lights looked like a big theater—with a stage, room for dancing and balcony seats. They served some food, but mainly liquor. The crowd was pretty much all-black, 95 percent black. It was a great dance club, for a while it was *the* dance club in that part of Dallas. And it was crowded, sometimes over 2,000 people would jam into City Lights on a hot Saturday night.

Music was the thing that brought people there. There was a deejay spinnin' stuff and lots of live music, too. New bands got a shot at playing there, and established acts, too. In fact, most any group that was passing through Dallas—before they got really huge, anyway—played at City Lights. *Everyone* at one time or another played there, from jazz and rhythm and blues acts like The Bar Kays, Confunkshun and Lakeside, and, of course, rap, from M.C. Hammer, to Rob Base and even 2 Live Crew. Just any name you can think of probably played City Lights at one time or another in the '80s.

I didn't know this at the time, but every once in a while they'd have talent contests at City Lights. It was an idea the owner and management had to help buck up business on slow nights when there wasn't a big name playing. They had the contests about twice a year—called 'em Star Quests.

Anyway, *anybody* could sign up, whether you were a singer, band, rapper, dancer or comedian, didn't matter. The contest was open to anyone. You'd get up on stage, be judged by a panel that included the owner and manager—but mostly by the reaction of the crowd, of course—and you could win musical equipment. They'd made a promotional deal with a local music store, and they had drum sets, keyboards, guitars and stuff to give away.

The biggest lure, though, was that they also promised that talent scouts from the big record companies might be in the audience. And every kind of entertainer, from rapper to rocker to band, was looking to get a record company interested. That's how careers start. And it wasn't just empty promises. Since City Lights was one of the most popular and well-known clubs in Dallas, reps from record companies *did* go there all the time. I should know!

What I didn't know was that I'd ever be entered in any kind of contest. It was the summer of 1987, and I'd been mostly hanging around Monopoly's. This friend of mine named James thought I was a pretty good rapper, dancer and beat-boxer. I didn't know that he talked to the owner of Monopoly's, a guy named Tommy Quon—who was going to have a *big* effect on my life—and asked him if I could perform there. Tommy was too busy to audition me right at that moment, so he suggested we go over to City Lights, which he also owned, where his manager, John Bush—another person who'd become very important in my life—was taking names for a big talent contest they were about to have. This friend of mine didn't tell me he'd had these conversations. I didn't realize we were heading over to City Lights so I could get signed up in some kind of contest!

We got to City Lights—it was my first time there— and I'm driving a cool car, my IROC-Z. I saw what kind of neighborhood it was in, so I parked the car right under the marquee, practically on the sidewalk. Later on, Tommy Quon told me that they wanted me to move it, but he decided not to hassle me about it. He said I walked in there looking like a movie star, like I had star quality about me even then, which I know sounds like a big-headed thing to say, but that's what Tommy says.

So anyway, we got there and my friend told me he's going to the bathroom. He came back a few minutes later, and showed me this white sheet and gave it to me. I looked at it and said, "What is this?" He said, "I just signed you up in a talent contest."

I was *not* happy. I said, "What talent contest?" And I looked around and it was real uncomfortable, 'cause all these people were already staring at me— a white guy in a predominately black club. And I thought, "Damn, I'm not getting up in front of all these people. I'm not getting up here." You know, I was scared as hell.

To them, I was in their territory, on their turf. And they looked at me as just a white boy probably looking for trouble. I felt like they were thinking, "What the hell's this guy doin' in here? Is he crazy?"

And then the contest started.

The first act got up there, and I hadn't even decided if I was going to do this yet. It was a rapper. I was getting really nervous, thinking again, I am *not* going to do this. But then my friend James said, "I dare you. Just go up when they call your name and do it." In all my life I've never said "no" to a dare.

But that wasn't the only reason I did it. As I'm watching this rapper do this thing, I realize—whoa, he's not that good. I'm starting to think, man, I can bust this dude! I can tear this dude up. I'll blow him away. And the crowd was going nuts over *him*—that's when I knew I was definitely going to go up there. I knew I could kill 'em on my lyrics. And as I'm getting more confident, my friend is egging me on. He's going, "Just do it. C'mon man, I dare you."

After the rapper, a band came up. They were taking 40 minutes just to set up. During that time, I went over to the guys who seemed to be in charge of the whole thing and told them I was definitely going to get up there. They said, "Fine, what do you need in terms of equipment?" And I said, "Just a microphone, man."

Then I went up to the house deejay and asked if he would spin this record for me called "Yeah Boy" by Rodney O and Joe Cooley. The deejay kind of looked at me strange. I felt like he was thinking, "*What* you want me to spin for you, white boy?" And so I told him, "Well, I rap. And I'm entering the contest, and this is the song I need." No way was he about to accommodate me. Not right off, anyway.

First of all, here I was, this new kid on his turf. He'd been the deejay there for four years and, like the rest of the crowd, really thought I was in the wrong place, or just crazy. But the other thing was that aside from being a deejay, he was a rapper, too. And whenever you put two rappers together in a room, it's inevitable that a battle's gonna start.

And that's what happened between me and this deejay, whose name was Earthquake—yep, yep, *the* very Earthquake, my deejay and chief musical collaborator right now. We're really tight now, but like I'm tellin' ya', we got off to a bad start.

Right away, he started putting me down—"Whoa, yeah, white boy's a rapper!" So I said, "Yeah, man, you wanna battle me or something?" So we battled in rap—right there in the deejay booth. And I was dropping him with my smoothest lyrics—I was killing him.

He was really getting angry, and we were just about to fight with our fists when the club's manager, John Bush, came into the booth to see what the commotion was about. That's the first time I ever met John. He said, "What's the problem here, fellows?" That's how he talks. When we told him, John ordered 'Quake to do it. He *had* to spin that record for me, 'cause that was his job.

I went down there on stage, and John Bush introduced me. He introduced me as M.C. Vanilla, 'cause, like I told you, that's been my rap name since seventh grade. And so I got up there, just me and my little microphone—they had this really serious sound system there, but I didn't use it, didn't need it—and I just did a rap off the top of my head.

This is true, the contest that changed my life and all. The rap I did wasn't even one I practiced before. It was all just off the top. I mean, by that time, after the duel with Earthquake, I was really into showing this crowd what I could do. I *lived* for the competition.

And I rocked! The only thing I had for a beat was clapping my own hands and, you know, urging the crowd to clap too. At first, they weren't clapping or doing anything 'cause they were all still in shock— "White boy going to try to rap?" They were actually laughing at first—not only the crowd, but the other M.C. who'd been up before me. They'd never seen me before, didn't know where I was from. And I'm thinking, "All right, laugh at *this*, man!"

And I busted a serious rhyme on their butts. I looked straight at the other M.C., that first guy up, who was standing right at the edge of the stage, and started off right away by dissin' him, goin', "You ain't about nothin', Jack. You can't get with Vanilla so you better step back!"

The whole crowd, everyone's jaws dropped open 'cause they knew I was dissin' their M.C. and that was really trippin' them out, that I had the nerve to do that. But they realized I was good, I was bustin' it, I was killin' them. The M.C. I was dissin' knew it first, and said, "Okay, you got me." As I continued, I even gave him and some of the others the chance to come back on stage and try to dis' *me*. But they're goin', "No, no, no, we can't touch this."

The crowd went nuts, and they *all* started to clap along with me, really loud, and I just kept on blowin' my raps at 'em. I don't remember exactly what I said, but I know I ended the last rap with the line, "I can even rock a beat, without a turntable." That's when I came in with my beat-boxing, and I knocked 'em dead.

The crowd was still clapping, and I was beat-boxing on the mic. It was just boomin' out into the room. I could see them just trippin' on me, thinking, "This boy is *jammin'!*" And I was just rockin' the house with my beat-boxing.

Then I took it up a tempo. I speeded it up and did this beat-box that I call the "Freddy Krueger," which nobody's ever done. I use a deep voice that I put into beat-box form. Then I did some other beat-boxes.

Since I used to battle people in the streets, putting my own special effects into it came naturally. Any good beat-boxer can do a beat, but not many put variations on the sound. I created another beat-box sound called the "Popeye." While I'm beat-boxing I do some scratching sounds with my mouth, and it sounds like the cartoon character, Popeye. I also did another different effect that I call "Sanford & Son," which sounds like I'm doing a drum sound under water.

The crowd couldn't believe it. They were just freaking out that I could kill 'em with the raps *and* beat-box like no one ever heard before. Soon I had them on my side. As I'm up there performing, they started a chant: "Go white boy! Go white boy! Go white boy!" Yep, yep, the same exact chant we use now in "Play That Funky Music." That's where it came from—my first night in the club, during the contest.

I mean, they were just goin' nuts, and I was really into it. I was feeling it, and so I said, "You heard me bust a rhyme, you heard me bust a beat, but check *this* out as I move my feet!" I said it just like that and that was the cue for the deejay to spin the record I asked for, "Yeah, Boy." I started dancing—I mean moving like they'd never seen a white boy move before. They were just going nuts, nuts, nuts! Everybody in the house was trippin'. They couldn't believe what they were seeing—a white boy who could rap, beatbox *and* dance, do all three and be good at all three. That just totally blew 'em away, man.

Naturally, I creamed the competition and won the contest hands down. I got instant respect from everyone, the people who worked there and the crowd. I was *the* thing at City Lights from that night on. In fact, after the contest, they invited me to keep coming back as a performer, just get up on stage every night and do my thing. John Bush put me back on stage every night the club was open. I didn't get paid, just got into the club free and got free drinks. You know, at that point, that was enough for me, because I was a star at this club. I loved the attention. All these people loved me.

Back to that first night, though. When I got off the stage, before I left, suddenly all these people, these guys that were there, started giving me their cards. They were from record companies. A guy from Warner Brothers was there, a guy from Motown, they were all there. I took the cards and put 'em in my pocket, went home and went to sleep. It's not that I wasn't excited about these record guys being interested in me, that this contest might lead to something, but I thought, "Ah, they're probably just teasing me, I'll never be a star." So I didn't take it all too seriously.

The next day, I got this phone call. In order to enter me in the contest, my friend had to put my phone number down on the entry form. The call was from Tommy Quon, the owner of the club. He told me that aside from owning City Lights and Monopoly's, he was also a talent manager. He said he wanted to sign me and manage my career. I was thinking, "Yeah, okay, I need a manager. I guess he's cool, he owns the clubs. He doesn't look like a guy who's just out to take the money." And he started telling me about other acts he manages, other deals he's making, that he's been in the business a long time, has a lot of connections and all. So I thought, "Okay, that's cool."

I signed with Tommy the very next day—fastest act he's ever signed! Probably the best move of both our lives!

First thing Tommy does is tell me my name's got to go. Vanilla M.C.—it's a good name for a white rapper, 'cause of my complexion and all. But Tommy thought there were already too many rappers out there using the "M.C." part—there was M.C. Hammer, M.C. Smooth, Young M.C., M.C. Shy. He thought I should be something different. So he thought for a moment and said, "You know, your raps, your rhymes are really *smooth*, smooth as Ice, in fact. How about Vanilla Ice?" And I thought, "Okay, cool." I mean, it wasn't any big deal, any big revelation. It sounded okay to me. So that became my new name, from that moment on.

What also started right about that time was that hip

people were suddenly adding the word "baby" to the end of their sentences. Radio deejays were doing it on the air, saying, "And that song was by M.C. Hammer, *baby!*" I mean, *everybody* was talking that way, ending sentences with baby. And before you knew it, when people were talking to me, or when I was up on stage, they'd be calling me, "Ice, baby."

Right at the same time, Earthquake—by now, we were cool—was working on this track, creating music for a new song. One day he came up to me and said, "Hey, Ice baby, what's going on?" Then as we were talking, he started calling me, "Ice, *Ice* Baby." That's how the hook came about. The track he was working on eventually became, of course, "Ice Ice Baby." He wrote the music and the hook, I added the lyrics. We collaborated on that about six months after I signed with Tommy, at the beginning of 1988. That's how long the song's been around. We didn't get into a studio to record it right away, though. That took a while.

In fact, everything took a while—much longer than I thought it should.

ICE CARVINGS

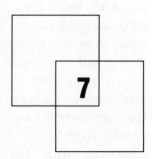

7

*"I'm not an M.C. who
comes here to play,
Yo, boy, I'm serious,
I'm goin' all the way."*

WHEN I SIGNED up with Tommy, I didn't know
what a manager actually did. I knew he owned the
clubs and had all these music biz connections. I knew
he worked with other acts, but I had no clue about
what's involved in all that. I wanted him to get me a
record contract. I wanted to make money and I wanted
to be famous. But I didn't know *how* he would go
about doing this. I found out real soon.

There's lots of steps, or links—as Tommy likes to
call them—to join together before you can try to sell
an act to a record company. The first step was working
on my music. I was good, but I was not polished. My
raps were good, but I needed more of them. My performing was good, but I needed to work on my timing.
My dancing, on the other hand, didn't need any work

69

at all. That I just developed on my own and no one ever had to work with me on that.

As far as the whole Vanilla Ice package goes—'cause that's what it is, any performer has to be packaged to some extent, has to have something about him that grabs people—that had to be created and worked on. And, like I say in "Ice Ice Baby,"—"Stop! Collaborate and Listen." That's exactly what Tommy and I did from the moment we got together—lots of listening and even more collaboration.

Part of Tommy's job as a manager was to bring in producers and songwriters for me to collaborate with. He started right away with a producer and songwriter named Kim Sharp. Kim used to be with the group Chocolate Milk. They had a hit called "Blue Jeans, Blue Jeans." He also played guitar for Prince on the *Purple Rain* tour. Since he often worked out of Dallas, Tommy knew him. Tommy knew practically everyone on the music scene in Dallas, and across most of the south, too.

Kim came in with a ballad he'd written called "I Love You," which is a real sweet rap with a sax solo on the end. We worked on it together—him on the music, me on the raps. We worked in hotel rooms, local studios, all over the place. Finally, it was ready. We rented time at Science Arts Recording Studio in Dallas and Kim produced it. That was the first song I ever recorded, and it's still on my *To The Extreme* album today.

It was great experience working with Kim and learning from him. But for another song, Tommy wanted to expose me to someone who was more into hip-hop. So he called a guy he knew from New York named David Deberry. It was Dave's job to come in and give me a tougher, grittier "New York" sound. David and

Kim worked together—and then I came in—on the song "Go Ill," which is now the B-side to the "Funky Music" single.

While all this was happening, Tommy was searching for other producers. He wanted me to collaborate with the best, and learn from them. I was pretty fast at picking things up. I really learned every step of the way.

One thing I had to deal with was learning how to be patient. That's never been my strong suit, but it is part of the creative process in this business. Everything takes more time than you think it should.

Another thing I learned is everything takes money. You can't just ask these producers and experts to come in from wherever they live and work with you for free. You've got to fly 'em in, pay 'em for their expertise. You got to put 'em up in hotel rooms and pay for studio time when you're ready to record. And you've got to pay for tapes and demos. Naturally, *I* had no money for this; Tommy paid for it all. He sunk a lot of his personal money into getting Vanilla Ice ready. That's one big reason I'm glad we made it—Tommy's finally getting his investment back, big time!

The third collaborator I worked with in those early days was Khayree Shaheed, another rap producer that Tommy got through one of his connections. Khayree came in with a song called "Hooked," but that wasn't his only contribution. We did *a lot* more polishing. Then we wrote "It's A Party" together. I wrote most of the lyrics, Khayree worked on the music. One of the best things he did was a rap version of the old Rolling Stones classic, "Satisfaction." That was really cool.

Khayree and I went into a studio called Luminous Sounds in Dallas, run by Paul Loomis, to record those three—"Hooked," "It's A Party" and "Satisfaction." Khayree did the main producing on them, but, like I said, I was learning every step of the way—not only from him, but from being exposed to what Kim and David did in the studio, too. That was a whole new world for me—one I got into real quickly. Now producing, or co-producing, is one of my favorite parts of making rap music. I was lucky, though, because even though these guys knew what they were doing, they let me learn from them and also took a lot of my suggestions. So I ended up having a pretty big hand in the producing of my album, which is unusual for a first timer.

While I was working with producers and in the recording studio, I was also spending a lot of time on my own raps and routines, plus rehearsing what I was learning. And every night City Lights was open, I performed there. I worked hard, and I always made a stir there.

At this point, City Lights was still a big club in Dallas, and all the rap and soul stars that came through performed there. That's when I became opening act for all of them. I would do just a couple of songs, 'cause I was really a "baby" act. But I did open for 2 Live Crew, N.W.A., Easy E, Rob Base, Rodney O and Joe Cooley—even Paula Abdul—she played at Monopoly's—and M.C. Hammer.

At first, most of the rappers didn't have any respect for me—until I got out there and did my thing. When I got onstage, busted the room with my show, it was a different story. It was like, "Damn! This homey is bad!"

The rapper Ice T told me, "You're gonna make it, Ice. You're gonna go." And M.C. Hammer wanted to sign me to his record label, Bust It Records. But

Tommy turned him down, 'cause he knew I wasn't really ready yet.

At the time, he just thought it would be better to stay in Dallas and keep workin' the way we were. I understand all that now, but when I heard that Tommy turned M.C. Hammer's people down, I was real mad. I remember confronting him: "Tommy, M.C. Hammer wants *me*—I-C-E! How could you say no?" But even back then, Tommy said, "Ice, you're gonna be bigger than Hammer. You're gonna be huge."

That's one of the most important things I had going for me—people like Tommy Quon who believed in me. If you don't have that, it's hard to ever go anywhere. And there was a time when it seemed like Tommy was the *only* person who believed in me. Everyone around him, except John Bush, was saying, "Forget it, he'll never make it." But we kept at it.

Tommy said that one of the reasons he knew I'd make it eventually was my attitude. Even though I was at the bottom of the totem pole at City Lights in those days, I always acted like a star. I had attitude and in Tommy's mind, "All the big ones have attitude." Even when other people would get mad at me and say, "This guy has a chip on his shoulder," Tommy felt it was important for me to feel I was the best.

The other reason Tommy kept the faith was that I was never booed at City Lights, even with the toughest audiences. I always got respect from the crowd, and Tommy felt if I could do that there, I could do it anywhere. Pretty soon, he was booking me into other clubs and larger venues around Dallas, where I opened for bigger names like Public Enemy and Tone Lōc. Performing every night, being exposed to pros like that, gave me a lot of experience. All the while, I kept on polishing my own act.

One thing Tommy learned from watching M.C. Hammer's career was that it *was* possible to "cross" rap over from the urban audience to a more mainstream one. Hammer did it. We thought my music would do it. And we worked towards laying the groundwork for that to happen.

I started collaborating with Earthquake on "Ice Ice Baby." With some help from rapper/producer M.C. Smooth, the three of us nailed that track down at Luminous Sounds Recording Studio. That was about the time I started getting a posse together. Everyone who came on to work with me is from Dallas, from 'Quake, to the dancers I hired, to the musicians—all of the original posse were put together there during this period.

All this time, Tommy kept bringing in even more people. The team of Wayne Stallings and Darryl Williams came in with a couple of tracks, "Ice Cold" and "Rosta Man." Another person who worked on "Rosta Man" was Craig Pride, the son of country singer Charlie Pride. But I wrote the lyrics on both of them. We recorded those at Sweet Taste Production Studios.

As we made our demos, we started shopping them around. We thought "Play That Funky Music" had the best shot. That was our single. We sent it out to record company people, A & R (artist & repertoire) people, our music attorneys in Los Angeles, anyone we could think of. The purpose of sending the demo out was to get a deal, to get a record company to sign me as a rap artist.

Everybody turned us down. Oh, there were a couple of companies that offered me a "single" deal—that is, they'd agree to distribute just that one single, with no commitment for an album. But that wasn't what we wanted. Besides, there's really no money in that, and we needed to start making some, to at least pay our expenses.

We'd keep trying, and we'd keep getting letters back from the record companies rejecting me, saying things like, "At this time, this artist is not right for us." Or, "This artist is a little too soft for us." Or, "Come back to us when you have some stronger material. What you sent is not what we're looking for." Like anything else, record companies are looking to represent a variety of different kinds of music on their labels. They have slots to fill and if you don't fill them, they turn you down.

It was *very* discouraging. But I kept on dancing and working. After about six or eight months of this, Tommy made what seemed like a drastic move—which was partly motivated by need. The area around City Lights, which was never good, was getting worse. Drugs came into the neighborhood and within a couple of months, the club really started going downhill. So Tommy abruptly closed City Lights down. Along with that move, he decided to put *all* his energy into music. He made a 100 percent commitment to trying to make his other acts work, and trying to make Vanilla Ice work.

His first step was to take matters into his own hands. If no record companies wanted his acts, he'd start his own record label. He felt that with his background in clubs, management, and promotion, it was a natural progression for him anyway. He called it Ultrax Records.

Tommy had all the know-how he needed to start the label. What he didn't have was a network set up to distribute the records Ultrax would be producing. He knew of a man named John Abbey, though, who had a record company named Ichiban, which was independently distributed. Tommy's idea was to link Ultrax up with Ichiban. It took him nearly a year to do it!

John Abbey had never heard of Tommy Quon and at first didn't even return his calls. Lots of other managers would've given up at that point and looked somewhere else. But that's what makes Tommy different. He believed that hooking up Ultrax and Ichiban was the right move—and refused to give up until he made that happen.

After several months, John Abbey began seeing Tommy's name in the record trades—mainly because of his other acts like Mac Band and Mikki Bleu. Finally, the two talked. Tommy told John he wanted to make a deal, but only for distribution. He didn't want his acts to be swallowed up by Ichiban, he only wanted to have Ultrax Records get to the record stores through Ichiban's system. Tommy was a marketing major in college and understood a simple rule: No matter how good the record is, no matter how many radio stations are playing it, if customers can't buy it, that record is nowhere.

Once the deal was made, we released the very first Vanilla Ice album. It was comprised of all the tracks I'd been recording with all the various producers. It had "Ice Ice Baby," "Play That Funky Music," "Go Ill," "I Love You," "Rosta Man," "Satisfaction," plus "It's A Party," "Dancin'," "Havin' A Roni," "Ice Cold," and of course, "Hooked."

When we made our deal with Ichiban and released our single and album, that's when things started to happen. At this point, the goal was to get airplay on radio stations. If a radio station plays it, then listeners have a chance to decide if it's good or not, and that's what we were looking for.

We had confidence that if people heard the music, they'd groove on it. But reaching that goal wasn't easy. It never is. Program directors of each radio station decide which records get played, and it's very hard to even convince them to *listen* to new records—they get hundreds a week. You're at a disadvantage, too, when you're on a tiny, regional record label. There's no money and no big guns to really push the song. Those are the realities of the record business—*man*, I was learnin' a lot!

But with our Ultrax/Ichiban connection, our luck was starting to change—at least a little. Some small radio stations around the south did play "Funky Music." It was something, but we weren't creating any momentum. The record wasn't suddenly jumping to the top of the charts and being picked up by other stations.

After a while we knew we'd have to do more to try and make this thing happen. We knew we'd have to take our act on the road.

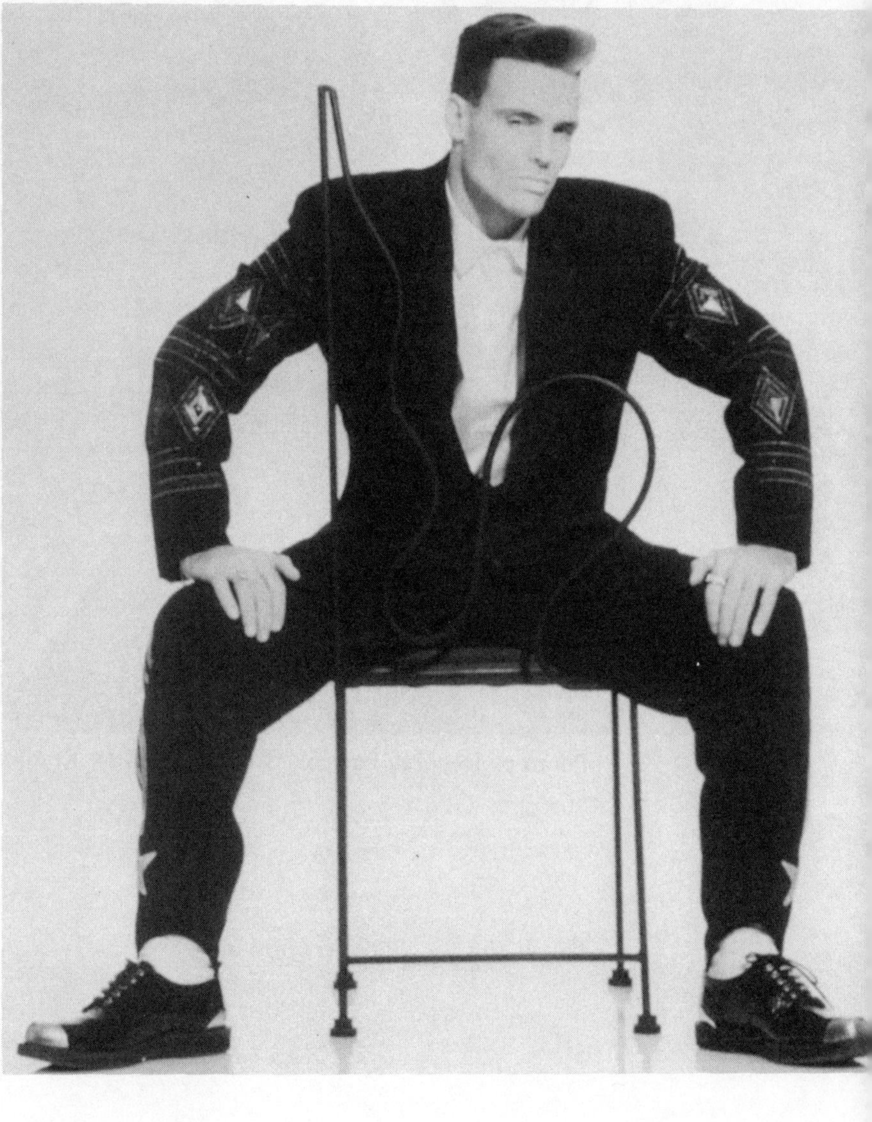

Photo by Deborah Feingold. Courtesy of SBK Records.

Photo by Deborah Feingold. Courtesy of SBK Records.

This is the Ice that you know now.

But this is Ice at 18...

...And then at 19 and gettin' chilly.

Who says I never won anything? These are only a few of the more than 400 motocross trophies that I've been awarded.

Motocross was my life for a lot of years. It was going to be my career.

Much of my confidence comes from my racing years. That's where I learned to just "go for it."

I loved winning, being in the lead, being number one.

Rappin's what I do now. My songs tell you who I am.

My dance style came from the street—I took what I saw there and improved on it.

Dancing is one of the things that I do best.

Photo © Todd Kaplan

You've made me number one!

Photo © Todd Kaplan

That's why when I give a concert I don't give 100 percent—I give 1,000 percent! When it's over, I'm beat.

Yep! Yep!

*And I am from Miami,
no matter what anyone
says.*

My VIP Posse: Me with Tommy Quon, my manager. Tommy's believed in me since the beginning.

My VIP Posse: Tommy, me, and Jerry Ade, owner of Famous Artists, my booking agency. They're the guys that get me to you.

Peter Seitz, my booking agent, got me my big break when he booked me as M. C. Hammer's opening act.

Charles Koppelma Chairman of SBK Records, gave me shot at the big-leag record biz.

My Road Posse: John Bush is my road manager and someone who knew me when, knows me now, and keeps me going.

My Road Posse: Aaron keeps things cool wherever we go and that's why we call him "Chill."

Dealing with the media is the toughest part of making it...

Photo © Pat Field

... That's why sometimes you just have to head home and chill.

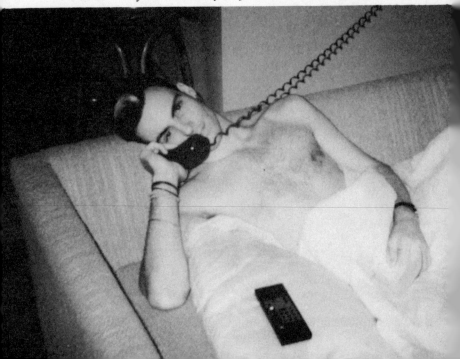

Old friends, best friends really help you keep it all in perspective. This is Darron Wehland, who's always been there for me.

Looking good and looking different—being out there on the cutting edge of style, setting styles—has always been important to me.

TO THE EXTREME

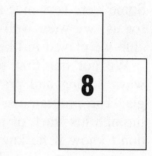

8

"Rhymes are clean,
there's no need to be ill,
And when I'm on the mic,
I let 'em all spill."

IT WAS TOMMY who realized that we really had to go out there and create something, get what's called a "buzz" going about Vanilla Ice, and about "Funky Music." We took a real "grass roots" approach.

We rented a van and squeezed six of us in—me, three dancers, a deejay and Tommy—*plus* our equipment and hit the road. Tommy set things up in advance. He called the few radio stations that were actually playing the single and told them that we'd come to their town and promote the record. We'd play in local clubs, we'd play in stores, we'd do whatever they asked us to do. Most of the stations just said, "fine." So Tommy hooked up a network of about 30 stations, from Dallas to Austin, San Antonio, Houston, and then swinging through Louisiana, Mississippi and Alabama. Then, we'd shoot up to Georgia, South Carolina, North Carolina, Virginia and make another loop back to Texas.

You wouldn't believe the dives we played! Some were clubs in the middle of nowhere with real country music families showing up. Others were in cities. Some were very nice and some were the pits. Luckily for us, we were well received in *all* of them. Every club we played in liked our act.

We got our first real break—the one you're always hoping and praying for—in Columbus, Georgia. The programmer there, Darryl Jaye, was going through his stack of records and for some reason—I don't know if he knew that Vanilla Ice was a white rapper or not—just decided to play my single. But instead of playing the "A" side, "Funky Music," he accidentally flipped it over and put on the "B" side, which of course was "Ice Ice Baby." He just put the wrong side on and suddenly really started grooving on it. The listeners decided they really liked it and began requesting it.

That station, WAGH, was the biggest station so far that played any song by Vanilla Ice—it had at least 100,000 listeners. And that's when the buzz that we hoped to create finally started. After all the requests started pouring in, Darryl Jaye knew his instincts were right and started pumping "Ice Ice Baby," played it 'round the clock.

It shot up to number one on WAGH and then, which was even better, in sales in the stores around Columbus. That's when we knew for sure that we really had a chance—when we realized that in that part of the country, anyway, we were outselling Madonna. This all happened in March, 1990. It had been a little less than three years since I won the contest at City Lights.

We went back on the road and did some more promotional gigs. We spent about four months out, in two different swings around the south. With Columbus, Georgia, as our anchor station, we went to Chattanooga, Tennessee, and got play and support from WJJT. The programmers there, Keith Landecker and Judith Stone, just took "Ice Ice Baby" and shot it up to the top. And this is without the politics of radio. It went to number one in airplay and again to number one in sales in that area, too.

Back home in Dallas, however, it was another story. Tommy tried, pleaded for months, to get the song added to the rotation of radio station 104—the one he did his advertising on. But they resisted—and so did every other radio station on our home turf. Talk about being bummed!

Anyway, at the start of the summer 1990, I did a concert there. After that, one of our other big stations, KJMZ 100.3, added it on in full rotation. Tommy had to beg for that one too—but as soon as the program director, Elroy Smith, saw my act, he said, "All right, I'll give you a shot." And when 100.3 went on it, that gave us real credibility, 'cause that's a major market. It's got over 500,000 listeners. After that, we got one more big station added to our "chain," Hot 95 in Jackson, Mississippi. Dave Morales was the guy there who believed in it.

With those four stations pumping it, "Ice Ice Baby" sold 40,000 copies within two months. And *then* record companies, the biggies, the majors that we'd tried to get before, started noticing Vanilla Ice—and wanting to make a deal with me. Even though we were on our own label, we still knew that to break through big time, we had to be with one of the majors.

Bill Deutsch from Atlantic Records said, "We want you on our label. Let's make a deal." And we were thinking about it seriously, when we heard from five or six other companies.

Each time we got an offer, Tommy would tell me about it. He even told me way back when we got those offers for just the one single. And every time I'd get so excited I'd say, "Let's take it, let's take it. C'mon, man, let's get a record." That was all I cared about.

But each time, Tommy would say, "No, we're not going to take it 'cause they're not offering us enough. They don't want to give us anything. We'll hold out."

So we kept holding out. Each time, I got mad at Tommy, and I'd yell at him, tell him he was wrong, tell him, "Let's just take any deal and sell some records and show them we can do it. I don't care if they don't want to give us any money up front, or if they agree to push the record or anything." I just wanted to have a record out. To myself, I thought, "Who cares if it sells or not, I can always go back to selling cars. I'm still going to have a record, with *my name* on it to play and impress girls." I didn't look beyond the moment.

Another thing Tommy and I disagreed about, the argument we kept having, was about the kind of image I wanted to put out. Coming from where I did, and having been through what I did, I was real tough—and I wanted to be the toughest rapper out there. If it were up to me alone, my stuff would be much more hardcore. 'Cause that's what I like and that's what I am. But Tommy convinced me that there were enough nasty rappers out there, that people were getting sick of that kind of stuff. We argued back and forth about that a lot, but I can see now that he was right.

He never tried to change my dance routines or, more important, my lyrics at all. But we did fight about what songs to record. "I Love You" was not one of my favorites. My favorite song from the original album was "Hooked." It's got a nice, hard edge, which is what I'm into. But Tommy's the manager and that's part of his job. Artistic direction is what it's called.

With all our disagreements, I know I'm lucky to have Tommy, because he really was the one who believed in me enough to see beyond the moment. He held out for the best and got it for me. And that was the deal with SBK Records.

It happened in July of 1990. We were negotiating with Atlantic when we hit a snag. Our attorney, Gregg Harrison, is with a firm in Los Angeles that handles Wilson Phillips and a lot of other big acts. Gregg was frustrated with Atlantic and asked his partner, Peter Lopez, who represents Wilson Phillips, if he thought SBK Records would be interested. Peter said, "They're a great company and would do a terrific job."

So Gregg called the head of the record company, Charles Koppelman, and pitched it to him. Charles took action immediately. He had his people check with key radio and sales people. He called Dave Morales at Hot 95, who told him that "Ice Ice Baby" was a real smash—and played it for him over the telephone! That was the first time Charles Koppelman heard the song. Based on that one listening, the reports from his people and his own instinct, Charles agreed to a deal within hours. By the end of the day it was a done deal. And it was probably one of the best deals they've ever made.

It turned out to be a great deal for me, but when I first heard about it, I didn't get too excited. After all the disappointments and the rollercoaster of things happening, looking good, then falling apart, by the time SBK came along, my feeling was, "Yeah, right. I'll believe it when I see it."

What turned out to be the best part of the deal was that SBK made me "top priority," which meant that my record wasn't going to sit at the bottom of the pile, just another one of their releases. They were going to do publicity, make a really big noise about "Ice Ice Baby," and try to get it played on the biggest radio stations all over. They had faith that as soon as all of America heard it, it was gonna go to number one. And, as I've found out, that's what makes it happen. Getting "top priority" almost guarantees your record's gonna be a hit, I don't care *who* you are. Only the major record companies can really do this for you, and SBK's in the major leagues. People have got to love the record, but once they do, the record company can push it to number one.

Right after I signed with them, I went into the studio. They wanted to use most of the tracks from *Hooked*, but felt we needed to add a few more. That was no problem. We added "Life Is A Fantasy," "Ice Is Workin' It," "Stop That Train," plus all the little musical "interludes" like "Yo Vanilla" and "Juice To Get Loose By."

We did have one big problem, and that was with "Satisfaction." We'd done a rap version for the *Hooked* album. But when the SBK deal came along, we wanted to take some of the original

Stones guitar track and use it—which, in rap, is called "sampling."

So we asked the Stones for permission to use it and they said, "No way." Instead of wasting time trying to figure out another way to use "Satisfaction," we just dropped it from the SBK release. Later on, as you probably know, we will be using it on a live album.

Anyway, we also needed to repackage the whole album under a new name. I picked *To The Extreme* as a title, 'cause that's what Vanilla Ice has always been about—taking *everything* to the edge, to the extreme.

Even though I had 100 percent faith in my music, I didn't think it would ever go to number one—not on the pop charts, anyway. I just didn't think the pop stations were really going to play it. I heard it on urban stations—that's the name the record industry uses for rhythm 'n blues or soul stations—but I couldn't believe it was going to cross over to pop. That's the only way to make it *really* big, though, 'cause pop outsells urban by something like ten to one.

So even though SBK was gettin' it out there, gettin' it played, I still never dreamed that "Ice Ice Baby" would go to number one on the pop charts. I knew I was finally getting my chance—I *dreamed* about havin' a number one song—but I didn't think it would actually happen.

All the while this was going on, Tommy was negotiating a deal with a new agent. An agent is the person who books your concert dates. We were at the point where we wanted some major bookings. We felt we were ready. Tommy had worked with a top music agent named Peter Seitz before, and they were real tight. But Tommy wasn't happy with the agency Peter worked for and wanted to switch. We made the move to Famous Artists—and took Peter with us. Peter was another real believer in the power of Vanilla Ice from the beginning. He worked like crazy to get me some good gigs, and it was through him that I got the best one of all.

In the summer of 1990, M.C. Hammer was on top, and when plans for his big tour were announced in the industry, *everyone* wanted to be on it, opening for Hammer. It would be incredible exposure! Peter and his supervisor were the ones who got me on that tour. Even though we were hooking up with SBK and "Ice Ice Baby" was out there, we still needed that exposure.

Peter had to persuade Hammer's manager—and brother—Louis Burrell, and the main tour promoter, Al Haymon, that I'd be right for the tour. He did it by convincing them that since "Ice Ice Baby" was gaining popularity on KMEL, a big market in San Francisco—Hammer's home turf—that I'd attract the same kind of audience he did. Peter and his supervisor pushed every second, he didn't let up until they finally said "yes."

I was *trippin'*, man, *really* excited about being on that tour. As it turned out, I was only on it for a few months, because when things started happening big time for me, I had to leave and get ready for my own headlining tour. But while I was out with him, I did learn a lot.

Bottom line, M.C. Hammer is one of the best entertainers and performers around, a real talent. Just from watching how he does things, how he puts on a show, I picked up a lot. And Hammer was always cool with me. He was always encouraging, and even when it looked like I might be able to "touch" him—

that is, knock him out of the number one spot—he never acted jealous or nothin'. In fact, he congratulated me—a real cool dude.

It was during the time I was on the Hammer tour that we went through the top. It happened so fast I barely knew it. I do remember the moment when I found out that I'd actually made it, made it really big, that is. I wasn't watching much TV or anything like that, and I didn't get to listen to the radio a lot—our tour schedule was really hectic. So I didn't know I'd gotten real popular. I found out when I went shopping at this mall, and I got completely attacked by like 400 people, and I was by myself! It was really weird. I could always go shopping by myself before, like anybody else, but suddenly, I had to find mall security guards to help me out. And when I wanted to go into a store, they'd have to shut the gate, lock the doors so people couldn't come in. It was just crazy. And that was the moment I knew, you know, "whew, this has gotten really big."

And it had. With the help of SBK, the Hammer tour and J. W. Sewell of Ichiban Records getting the "Ice Ice Baby" video on Video Jukebox Network and MTV airing it, "Ice Ice Baby" shot to number one on the Billboard Hot 100 charts. It happened in October, and it was the first rap single to ever do it.

It was certified gold and platinum simultaneously—which means it sold over a million copies—and, bottom line, made history. And not only U.S.A. history. "Ice Ice Baby" hit number one on the European charts soon after—in England, France and Germany. It hit the top in Australia and Japan, too. Blows my mind.

To The Extreme did even better, which is incred-

ible. It sold five million copies in the U.S. alone in
its first twelve weeks out. It was certified gold,
platinum, double and triple platinum on November
19, 1990. Didn't stop there—went to quadruple
platinum the next *day!* As of this writing, it's sold
over seven million copies, and it's still happening—
all over the world. It reached the Billboard Top 10
in five weeks—fastest debut album in all of 1990.
It spent ten weeks at number one. And yeah, it *did*
knock Hammer's LP, *Please Hammer Don't Hurt
'Em*, out of that spot. Word!

A lot of people have a lot of theories about my
success. Some say it's because I'm white, which I
think is total bull. I believe that with the same songs,
written and performed the same way, and with the
same record company support, anybody of any color
could've done the same thing. I think I'm good, won't
deny that. But I don't think my success has to do with
the color of my skin.

Other people say that my rap is clean and that people
were sick and tired of dirty words in raps, and that's
what made my stuff go over the top. They say that it
was time for something clean, and that's why Hammer
and I made it. It's true that we both deliberately made
records that were for a mainstream audience—but,
even though I *do* prefer harder stuff, I never felt I
needed to curse to express myself in rap. Yes, I did
make compromises, but I didn't change to become
successful.

It took me three long years of hard work and lots
of disappointments. I did everything I could and, for
a time, it really seemed that no one wanted to give me
a chance. We kept at it—pursuing resolutely—and in
the end just looked to God, and God gave us the break.

I hope I always remember that success is not man-made. It's something that you work hard for, but it's the Lord that takes care of you. I put myself with Him, and that's why *I* think I made it after all.

ICE ON RAP

9

". . . It's a foundation of breaks,
put to a beat,
Strong as concrete,
'cause I'm rockin' the beat!"

MY HEART IS in rap music and always will be. Rap music is lyrics, it's poetry with a beat. Rap music is about expression and that's how I express myself. Rap music is the expression of a whole generation of kids, the "under 25" generation who got turned on to it, just like I did, when "Rapper's Delight" came out.

That was the first commercial rap song, and we heard it on the streets before radio got hip to it. We were in high school, or junior high school, and it was the *first* music that was ours alone, just like rock was for a lot of older people. That's why I think that a lot of critics who are over 25 put down rap music. They really don't understand it, and they don't understand what it means to us. They don't really know what they're talking about.

No matter how much they put it down, though, rap music is here to stay. Yeah! Make that, hell, yeah! It's like when rock 'n roll first came out, people said *that* wasn't here to stay—it was a fad. But it stayed, just like rap will. And just like rock 'n roll changed over the years, rap will change, too. No doubt about that. It *has* changed already.

It's not just beats and rap anymore, it's a lot more musical. You need a lot of talent to come up with a hit rap record now. Years ago, it didn't take that much. But the people who started it are getting a lot more musical experience and studio knowledge—they're taking rap a lot more seriously than they did before. It's not just throwing a few rhymes together, it's technical and musical know-how, too.

Rap music is special because it's got so much soul. In my opinion, there would be no rap music without James Brown, the "Godfather of Soul." He's not a rapper, but he's got so much soul. His song "Funky Drummer" has been used a thousand times over—not only in rap, but in other kinds of music as well. Recently, George Michael slowed "Funky Drummer" down and used it in one of his new songs. But that's really James Brown, all the way.

Just like soul, rap music is so danceable, you can't sit still. Not only is it danceable, and listenable, understanding the words is the fun part. It's just so much fun, so cool. It's what's hip. Rap music is the hippest form of music there is, period.

Rap music is from the streets. That's where the form originated, and *real* rap music will always be from the streets. Like the blues, like funk, rap is black music.

I'm a white guy doing rap music—which doesn't mean I'm here to take it out of the streets. It means I'm a white guy who happened to grow up in the streets. That's where I learned to express myself, and rap is *how* I learned to express myself. A lot of people have problems with that. They see a white guy doing it and think, "There's no way he could know the streets; this is all a put-on." But they're wrong.

I don't even *see* skin colors. I hate skin colors. I wish the whole world was color blind. If the whole world was blind, there wouldn't be racism. Nobody would have any problems with Vanilla Ice, nobody would care where he's from or anything like that. The way it is now, though, people make assumptions because I'm white. And I don't dig that at all! Huh! I've been called a fake, a rip-off, all kinds of ugly names. People say I want to be black. I know who I am and I don't want to be anyone else—just Vanilla Ice, a guy who raps.

So the next thing people say is, "Well, now that Vanilla Ice has made it, a lot more white rappers are going to follow." That might seem like a natural assumption, but it's a wrong one. Not many white kids grow up on the streets. Not very many at all. So I just don't see a lot of really legit white rappers comin' down the pike. There will be copycats, yes, but successful ones, no.

My only problem with being a white rapper and having the image I do is that I don't get the respect of a lot of other rappers. They don't give me credit, because all they see is the image—which, as I said before, is a lot softer than *I* really am. They see me on the pop radio stations and automatically think Vanilla Ice is soft. They say the same thing about M.C. Hammer, they dis' him too, say he's too soft. It's because we both had number one albums that crossed over to the pop charts.

But the actual fact is that *personally* I'm a lot harder,

a lot more hardcore than that. I can write hardcore raps, and I can bust any M.C. out there. It's only when they get to know me that they realize that. So if they haven't seen me perform, or haven't met me in person, they don't give me a whole lot of respect. Even though a lot of rappers might not have respect for me, I do listen to their music and I like a lot of it: Audio Two, Big Daddy Kane, Eric B. & Rakim, Geto Boys, NWA. You might never have heard of these groups because they're not mainstream, but they are hot. And they *should* be getting more respect from the music world.

Rap music gets a *bad* rap for something called "sampling," which is the practice of picking up lyrics and music from other songs and using them strategically in original rap songs. Every rapper does it. I used David Bowie's and Queen's "Under Pressure" in "Ice Ice Baby," and Wild Cherry's "Play That Funky Music" in my rap of the same name. Hammer borrowed Rick James' "Super Freak" in "U Can't Touch This." Sampling has always been part of rap music and always will be. It's just part of the art form.

Now some people scoff at it and say, "Well, geez, all you gotta do is take an old song and twist it around and you can have a rap song. Where's the creativity in that?" But I don't look at it like that. The way I look at it, sampling is not only a creative thing, it's also a good thing. What we're doing is helping to bring back a lot of good music that either wasn't appreciated before or has been forgotten—like "Under Pressure." On the American charts, it only topped off at number 26, never went higher. But "Ice Ice Baby" went to Number One. So a lot more people are getting to hear it and appreciate it.

As far as creativity goes, I might be using a little bit of someone else's music, but I do put *my* touch to it. I write my lyrics, I produce most of my stuff, I help with the remixes—what's that if not creativity? I didn't just take an old song and sing it differently. That song "Under Pressure" never would have come back by itself. So instead of knocking rap, people should appreciate it for bringing back the older songs to a younger generation. It's a way for music to circulate. So the artist who originally wrote the song should be proud.

Now it's a different story altogether with Alpha Phi Alpha, the black fraternity. Someone said I stole their chant and used it in "Ice Ice Baby." That isn't true at all. "Ice Ice Baby" was written three and a half years ago—I had no idea what an Alpha was, I didn't know anything about it. It was the weirdest thing 'cause everybody kept coming up to me and saying, "Did you get this from the Alphas?"

I had never heard of them and never knew they had a chant with the words "ice, ice, baby" in it. So I'm thinking, "Wow, cool, big coincidence." The funny thing is, I heard from the guys in the fraternity and *they* don't seem to think I stole anything from them. In fact, they called up and said, "Yo, Ice, we're an Alpha fraternity at the University of Arkansas, and we want to use your song and your dance steps in our shows. Is that okay?" And I said, "Sure, you know, rock it!" So there wasn't a real controversy there, only what some critics made up. That one didn't have anything to do with sampling or stealing or anything. It had to do with coincidence.

Now just because rappers do use sampling doesn't mean we don't have to give credit—and money—to the original artists. No matter how you look at sampling—good, bad or indifferent—bottom line is yes, I did use somebody else's music and of course they've got to get credit for it and get paid for it. Rappers still have to look at sampling from a legal standpoint and get things cleared first. Fair's fair.

But the critics better get used to it: Sampling, like rap music, is here to stay. No one's gonna be able to kill rap music, no matter what they do.

Another thing about rap music: Everybody thinks they can do it. Everybody thinks it's easy to sit down and write a rap song, no big deal. They are so wrong. Rap is an instrument by itself. It's a form of poetry *and*—get this—it's a lot harder than writing a song. With a song, you can just throw in stuff, even if it doesn't make any sense, throw in meaningless sylla-bles. In rap you can't do that. You can't throw in a "Whoa, baby," just to make it end on a beat. You *have* to rhyme.

I'm not sayin' this because I can't sing. I *can* do straight singing, I do have a good voice. But I can't express myself through singing like I can through rap. With rap, I can let me be *me*. Singing doesn't do it for me. That's why even though a lot of people want me to sing, I won't do it. My heart is in rap music, and I won't do anything else.

Of course, I do think that my rap is different from most of the others. A lot of what's out there sounds exactly the same. You can't tell one rapper from an-other. *I* don't sound like L.L. Cool J or Big Daddy Kane or Run-D.M.C. I sound like Vanilla Ice.

Also, with a lot of rap, you really can't tell what they're rapping about. You listen and you go, "Wha-a-a-t? What'd he just say?" And then the next artist, or next song, comes up with the beats sounding almost the same, and you can't tell the difference. Even if the beat's real groovy and you can dance to it, if you don't know what was said, you're not getting much out of it.

With my songs, you can always tell what I'm saying. I tell stories in rap form. You can write a book from any of my raps, make a movie from my raps. I tell it from start to finish, you can sit there and listen to it and understand the whole story. Every song I have, except for "Dancin'," you could make a movie about. "Dancin'" was just made for getting up and moving. It's a party song. But as for all my other ones, there's nothin' in my raps you can't understand.

A lot of my raps are pretty much sexual, I won't deny that. But that's just me, expressing myself. When you buy Vanilla Ice, you get Vanilla Ice, not like New Kids On The Block. I'm not dissin' them, 'cause New Kids are great. They're very talented, very few groups can sell 21 million records, very few people can do what they've done. But when you buy New Kids, you're not getting what's in their heads, because, for the most part, they don't write their stuff. You're getting what's in Maurice Starr's head. They sing it, they're not Milli Vanilli, but except for the raps that Donnie Wahlberg wrote, you're not getting what's on their minds. With Vanilla Ice, you're getting what's on my mind. You're getting it all. So as far as the sexual stuff goes, well, I'm 23 years old, I'm single . . . I'm healthy, I'm interested!!

There's no question rap *is* going in a more mainstream direction, though. Radio is getting more involved because the fans are getting more involved. And I will say that part of the reason for my success is that I am helping to bring rap to a wider audience. Not just because of the record company being a mostly pop label, but also because of what I choose to put

out. I *can* do dirty raps, and I *can* put much more dis'
in rhymes, but I choose not to.

What I put out is the stuff that sells, the stuff that
most of the world likes. I use my brains and the advice
of my manager in deciding what to put out, 'cause,
as I said before, my personal favorite *is* the more hardcore stuff. I like gettin' nasty because, let's face it,
you can think of a lot of four-letter words that rhyme
off the top of your head. So it's easy, easier than
coming up with clean stuff. But now I got all forms
mastered.

You can either have the hardest stuff out there, and
get the respect from all the rappers in the world—
'cause when you do, they won't touch you, they won't
dis' you or nothin'—or you can come out with a clean
rap that America wants to hear, and wants their kids
to hear. You can come out with stuff that they can
play on the radio and everybody can hear it. It's a
choice you make. You can sell a few albums and get
a lot of respect from the rap community, or you can
sell a lot of albums and get respect from the rest of
the world.

I've chosen to bring rap to the rest of the world.
Nobody else was doing it before. I made it real clean,
and I made it so you could understand it. My stuff's
real smooth—"Stop! Collaborate and *Listen!*" You
can understand every single word. I don't slur any
words. I'm not illiterate. I've done a lot of learning
since I dropped out of high school.

And my stuff is catchy. All my songs are catchy.
Got to make a catchy song, one that, after the first
time you hear it, stays in your head, can't get it off
your mind, and it grows on you. I try to make my
lyrics easy to memorize, real simple. So everybody
knows all the words—which is great when I'm in

concert. It gives the whole audience a chance to sing along.

Speaking of writing raps, it's hard for me to say exactly *how* I do it. I get inspired to write at different times—sometimes the feeling just comes to me. I grab little scraps of paper, whatever's around. You wouldn't believe what hit songs were started on little memo pads by the phone in hotel rooms. I write in airplanes, on the tour bus, in the shower, walking the stairs. Raps come right into my head especially when I'm driving my car, when I'm by myself.

When I get in the mood to write, I sit down and write four songs at the same time. What'll usually happen is that I start off doing one and go, "Oh, that's a bad-ass idea." Then another line will come to me, but it doesn't match the song I've just started. So I start a whole complete *new* song. Then, I'll get to a certain point in the new song and get an idea for another one. So one thing kind of sparks another. It always happens that way. Then I'll leave it for a few days, come back to it and start all over, maybe from the second verse or something. Writing four songs at a time is basically the way I do it.

Right now, I've got about 300 pages of just raps. Tons of them, stacks of them, probably that I'll never use. Some people write when they're really bummed out, to help them get through whatever it is—but not me. I write mainly just for fun. I mean, I might write if I'm angry about something—like I wrote a few lines about the *press*, which we'll talk about in a few chapters—but for the most part, it's pretty upbeat stuff, so far, anyway.

I'm always thinking of different beats, which is also part of writing a rap song. And when I change the beat on something I've written, it changes the mood of the song—and that affects the lyrics. So I've got to go back and change them, too.

I write mainly about stuff that's goin' through my head, but it's got to be something I feel strongly about, not something trivial. I get into raps that make stories, that you could make a book out of. Right now, my raps are about fun things, but as I get older, who knows? Whatever I get into, whatever I get passionate about, that's what you'll find in Vanilla Ice's raps.

I don't play any instruments, except for a little piano. But I *do* go into the studio and produce, or co-produce, almost all my stuff. I work the sound board, I do the mixes and I am in total control of all aspects of my music. I know how it should sound and I pretty much direct everyone else that's working with me. I know my parts and everyone else's too. And bottom line, whatever I say goes: It's *my* music.

Same thing with the dancing. I choreograph all of it, my moves and the moves of the dancers, too. I dare anyone to say that someone else taught me my moves—that's always been my strongest suit. I audition the Vanilla Ice dancers, I hire them. I even taught Jay—that's Hi Tec—how to dance! In the beginning, he wasn't getting off to a quick start. Even Tommy asked why I was keeping him on. But Hi Tec's a friend, and you don't dump a friend. There's a lot of loyalty in the Vanilla Ice organization, you'll see that. Jay turned into one incredible dancer—anyone who sees him onstage knows that!

I'm tough on my dancers, too, because it's real important to me that the grooves and the moves are just right. If the dancers aren't keeping up, I have been known to blow up at them. But when it comes down to it onstage, we are *hot*, we are *the best*. That's hard work and professionalism—puttin' on the best shows for our audiences.

I have a lot to say about what goes on in my videos, too. So far we've done four of them, for "Ice Ice Baby," "Play That Funky Music," "Stop That Train" and "Satisfaction." I'm into doing the videos, 'cause they're like little movies—you get to express the words of the song visually. And no question that it was the video for "Ice Ice Baby" that helped the song cross over.

The "Ice Ice Baby" video was shot in Dallas. All the scenes you see, the graffiti, are in Dallas. The "Funky Music" video, which is a concert scene, was also shot in Dallas. But "Stop That Train" was done while we were in Canada. We did it in Montreal and Toronto. This one's more of a movie, not a concert scene. It's about a girl that's gettin' into some crazy games, and I'm saying, "Stop the train, this is too much for me, I want to get off." That's the point of the song, and you see it in the video.

VIPS

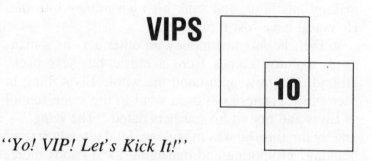

10

"Yo! VIP! Let's Kick It!"

NO ONE GETS to the top alone—no matter how good you are. You need support. And I've been lucky, because I've been supported by the best. So here's the chapter where I-C-E, that's me, gets to say "Thanxx" to the people who've been there, who believed and who helped make it all happen.

TOMMY QUON

Gotta start with him, first and foremost, because he's the one who got me here. He's my manager, and he believed in me from the get-go. I think you can see by now, Tommy did not give up. It took us three years to break, and all that time people told him Vanilla Ice would never work. Record companies told him, radio programmers told him, promoters told him, *everyone* in the music biz said a white rapper would never work.

But Tommy believed in me and stuck with it. We went through some hard times together. He invested money in me, and for a long time it didn't look like he was going to get it back. You know, that's unusual for a manager. A lot of them won't make the financial commitment. They'll wait for an act to start making money and then they'll say, "Hey, I want to manage you." But Tommy took the chance when I wasn't making anything, and sunk his own money into me. He could have lost it all.

In fact, he *has* lost money on other acts he's managed. Tommy comes from a music business background. He grew up around the whole Elvis thing in Memphis, Tennessee—even went to the same school as Elvis and one of his teachers dated "The King"— and by the time he was in college, he'd already started booking, promoting and managing local bands there. Later, he opened up a few dance clubs in Memphis. When he moved to Dallas in the late '70s, he started City Lights and then Monopoly's Park Place.

Through his background in promotion and booking groups for his clubs, both in Memphis and Dallas, Tommy developed a music network—he knew people in all phases of the biz, all around the mid-south area. During the '80s, he took on lots of groups to manage, like Out Of The Blue, The Mac Band, Don Diego, Mikki Bleu, I can't even remember them all. Some of them had regional hits and some success. But win or lose with them, Tommy learned a lot—which ended up helping me a lot.

There's a lot involved in managing someone's career, and Tommy does a lot for me. I already told you how he got me going, how he held out for the best deals and all that stuff. There's been a lot of "career counseling" and guidance, too. I might not always agree with Tommy, but I usually end up listening to him. He's been pretty dead-on right so far!

Tommy runs the business end of things from his company, QPM Inc., in Dallas. He's got a great staff there—the whole organization is like one big family. And I know that I might not always be the easiest person to work for, but they are workin' hard for me!

Aside from career stuff, though, Tommy's kept my head on my shoulders more or less, kept my ego in check when that had to be done. He's kept reminding me that "what goes up must come down," and that's something I've got to remember. He's a religious man and a family man—and most important, a good man.

Bottom line—I could not have made it without Tommy. That is how I feel.

BYRON MINO

I don't have a father, but I've got two people in my life who are father figures. One of them is Byron Mino.

Byron married my mom when I was eight, and even though they're not married anymore, he never stopped being a Vanilla Ice *and* a Robby Van Winkle supporter. He took care of me in lots of ways—especially financially—like helping me get my car and stuff like that. He cared about what I was doing, if I was in school, if I was in trouble. He tried to keep me as straight as possible, which wasn't too easy. But whatever I did, he always let me know he was there.

Byron's the kind of guy who'd tell us—me, my brother and our little sister—things like, "A man can make money, but money can't make a man." That's the kind of man Byron is. He's always worked hard his whole life, but he never cared about being rich. Byron's priorities are family and God.

And he lets me know, every day of every week, that with or without money, with or without Vanilla

Ice, he loves me just the same. He's completely cool
that way. I've learned that when you get this hot,
everyone wants to be your friend, everyone acts like
they love you. It's hard sometimes to tell who's for
real and who's just along for the ride: Byron's for real.

JOHN BUSH

Officially, John Bush is my road manager. But un-
officially, he's a lot more. He's the other "father figure" in my life.

John was one of the first believers, one of the first
people to encourage Tommy to take me on and another
one who kept pushing, trying to crack Vanilla Ice.
John used to make videos of me performing at City
Lights and shop 'em around to show music people
what I could do.

These days, when I'm on the road, he's with me,
24–7. And, believe me, *that* ain't easy! John Bush
takes care of everything on the road. He handles all
the press—anyone and anything that comes to me has
to go through him *first*. He sets everything up. He's
on top of every detail.

When you ask me where we're going next and what
time I have to be places, I don't know any of it—*he's*
the one who knows it all. He tells me what time I need
to wake up and what I have to do all day long. By
doing that job, he takes a lot of stress off my head.
There's no way I can concentrate on the shows and
the music if I have to deal with all that other stuff,
too. I'm lucky I have someone like John to do it.

I feel close to John personally. He's not only a father
figure to me, he's the whole posse's father. All of us out
here are still kids in a way, and we still need guidance.
John, like Tommy, is also very religious and family-

oriented, and he teaches us by example. He advises me and keeps me straight. I ask him for advice on all kinds of things, and he tells me straight up. We never lie to each other. We've got a real solid bond.

PETER SEITZ

Peter's the agent who books Vanilla Ice on tour, and who, as you know, helped get me aboard with M.C. Hammer last year. Peter's been an agent for a long time—he's also a musician, so he understands that mentality—and he's a key man on the Ice team. He's another believer from way back. That's why we brought him along when we changed booking agencies. Now, he's with the best booking agency there is, Famous Artists.

For business stuff, Peter's the best booker there is, bottom line; for personal stuff, he's cool to chill with. We're both pizza freaks and whenever we're together, we head for the best pizza in town. You never saw two dudes who could spend so much time talkin' about pizza—almost as much as we spend eating it. We're real serious about it.

CHARLES KOPPELMAN

Charles Koppelman is the "K" in SBK Records— the *man*, if ya' know what I mean. He signed me to his record label, which is now the hottest record label in the world, with me, Wilson Phillips, Technotronics and a whole bunch of other success stories.

He signed me based mostly on instinct and by listening to my record over the phone, which proves he's got real good instincts. He made a great deal for me and, along with the staff at SBK, is really responsible for pushing Vanilla Ice over the top. He's cool and has a lot of happenin' stuff planned for me—I'm ready!

GREGG HARRISON

Gregg's the legal eagle who's worked with Tommy for a long time. When he joined Lopez & Gonzalez (now it's called Lopez, Gonzalez & Harrison), a high-powered and respected L.A. law firm, he steered us over to SBK, which was a great move.

Gregg and everyone at Lopez, Gonzalez & Harrison work real hard for me, they've been through a lot with us. They're cool and on every special occasion, like my birthday, send me a little gift—gave me a professional masseur one time. They always write me letters, let me know they're there for me, on my side legally, working on my behalf.

JERRY & JOHN ADE

These brothers own Famous Artists, the best music booking company in the world. They're real cool. They have everyone from Rob Base to The Cover Girls, Ninja Turtles and New Kids On The Block as clients. They know the rock and rap scene and they're young enough to really get into it. They're not just suits who sit behind the desk and make phone calls. They get out on the road, they listen and do the best for me.

DANIEL GLASS & KEN LANE

These are the guys who headed up SBK's promotional team and they are truly at the top of their field in *that* game. Because they're so good, they give SBK Records an edge over the other companies. They believed in "Ice Ice Baby," and helped break it—I have to thank them for pushing Vanilla Ice over the top. They both deserve raises and promotions!

QPM

That's the name of Tommy's company in Dallas and he's got a support staff there who really work hard for me and do a great job. Terry Quon, Lynn Fallows, J.W. Sewell and Rickey Richardo put in the time and the effort—above and beyond the call of duty—and even though I might not always show it, I *am* glad to have them on my team.

EARTHQUAKE

His real name is Floyd Brown. He's from south Dallas, and he's the person who collaborates with me most on the music end. He's my deejay and he scratches my back.

We met back at City Lights the night of the contest, which I already told ya' about. So you know we started off as rivals, with me challenging him on his turf. But we're tight now.

We work together on the music all the time. He produces and I produce. He comes up with some beats and says, "Hey, Ice, check this out." I check it out and it's always slammin'. Once he came to my car, threw a tape in with three or four cuts he'd been working on, just *beats*, 'cause that's what he does best. I said, "Let's go to the studio, this stuff is totally slammin'!" Then I put lyrics to it. That's how we work together.

'Quake is the best deejay there is. He understands me more than anybody else does. He can read my mind. We'll be onstage and I don't have to say *any-thing* or signal anything to him, and we're both automatically thinking the same thing, like "Maybe this song should end right here." We both just *know* it's gonna end right there on a certain beat, and we just do it together—without any words or planning. That's good, solid stuff, man—can't go messin' with that combination.

HI TEC

His real name is Jay Huffman and, as you know by now, he's one of my dancers. I met Jay about four years ago in Dallas—met him in a fight, not against each other, against somebody else—and he's probably the closest person to me in the posse. He's my homey. We're real tight on a personal level.

Jay and I came up together in the whole Vanilla Ice thing. He was a good dancer, but I brought him along and now he's a great dancer. We work hard together—I want the dancing to be exactly right each time—but when it's time to play, we do that hard together, too. Jay keeps up with me, late nights, parties, all that fun stuff. We relate on the same level—we're both from the streets, but we're out of them for good now.

JUICE

Juice is also one of the Vanilla Ice dancers, one who's been with me for a while. Juice's real name is Marc Grinage, and he came along just at the right time.

He used to dance for the Dallas radio station 100.3, but I met him in a club at a dance contest. When I needed somebody experienced who could learn routines and learn 'em real quick, I thought of Juice. I auditioned him and he made the cut. Juice and I have been through some stuff together. We don't always agree on everything, but we always find a way to work it out. He respects me and I respect him.

E-ROCK

Even though E-Rock, who's also known as Everett Fitzgerald, is no longer one of my dancers, I can't leave him out of this book. He came up with me, we've been through tough times and good times together, and he's one of my homeboys, too.

I met E-Rock right around the same time as Juice, only a few days later. Same thing, I needed experienced dancers quick and E-Rock was hired. It was his choice to leave. I didn't want him to, but he's hooked on his woman, which I can understand, and didn't want to spend so much time on the road. I wish him good luck. I'm sorry he left, but I can dig it.

CHILL & BIG E

Security's real important when you're on the road as much as I am. I've got two bodyguards who are friends as well. Aaron Martin likes to be called "Chill," and Earnest Ellis goes by "Big E." If I call him Earnest, he gets so mad at me! Both of 'em are my homeys, I hung out with them a lot before we actually kicked Vanilla Ice off. I'm completely cool with them around, don't have to worry about anything.

GAIL "SKY" KING

Gail's my remixer and newest co-producer, too— she is the best, the king. I was driving in my car listening to this totally hot remix of a song called "Do The Right Thing" by Red Head Kingpin—and it was the best remix stuff I ever heard. I saw her name on the label and said, "Man, this is a *bad* girl, this is a *bad* remixer."

So when the record company asked me who I wanted to use as a remixer, I said one name and one name only. And they mentioned a whole bunch of names, saying, "You know there's a whole bunch of people who want to work with you." I said, "I don't care, I got who I want. I got the King." She's very talented, she's super great.

TONEY GONZALEZ & ALLEN LAWS

Just want to give some credit to the guys who come out on the road with me and make the Ice machine run smoothly. Toney's the techno-wizard, settin' up the drums and stuff like that. Allen we call the "Funhouse Mixer." He's the sound guy. We need 'em both and they're there for us.

BEST FRIENDS & FAMILY

Here's as good a place as any to acknowledge my best friend, Darron "Squirrel" Wehland, my brother by word and the craziest guy you'll ever know. Darron and his whole family are the best. Also, to Kip, my older brother, and his family: Thanx, dude.

AND . . . THE MAN UPSTAIRS

And most of all, of course, I thank God above, 'cause without faith in Him, there's nothing. Yep, yep!

ICE IS WORKIN' IT

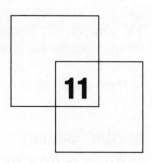

11

*"I saw my style, my soul
up on the dance floor . . ."*

MAN, I *love* being on the road. I love being on tour—which is a good thing, because as a performer you need to bring your act to the fans. You need to do it live—that's where you prove yourself, up onstage. That's where you know if you're any good or not, the crowd will tell you.

I've been performing my whole life, starting in the streets of Miami. But in the last three and half years I've been *everywhere*, all over the whole entire United States, every city. I've been to Europe—and this year I'm going to Japan and Australia, too. It's a trip and a half.

It's funny, though. At first all I wanted to do was get away from home, get out there and show everyone what I could do up onstage. But then when I'm out there for five, six months at a time, I can't wait to get home. I miss it so much. The weirdest thing is that

113

once I am home, I just want to turn around and go back out.

One thing you don't get out on the road is bored—there's always something happening, *always*, every day, every night. You never have a day where you wake up and go, "Huh, wonder what I'm gonna do today." You never go, "Well, I think I'll just watch TV tonight, sit home and chill." You know something's gonna be happening, something's gonna be going on.

Here's a taste of Vanilla on the road!

GETTING AROUND

We move from gig to gig, city to city, by bus. We don't do the plane thing, unless we're going overseas. But we've come a long way, baby, from the days when it was six of us—plus equipment—crammed into one tiny van. We upgraded to a real rock star tour bus when we got on the Hammer trip, which was cool, but it was still crowded: eleven of us rode together for the first half of that tour. Later, we added another one, the Star Bus, and were able to spread out.

Now we're doing it right. On my *To The Extreme* tour, we've got *five* tour buses for the crew and posse, and three 18-wheelers just to haul the equipment. We've got about 40 to 50 people out with us, including the people who set up the stage, take it down, move the stuff from city to city. We've got sound people, light people, wardrobe people and others who just help unload the trucks at each stop. And that's just the crew!

I ride on the Star Bus—for obvious reasons! But I'm not alone. John Bush, 'Quake and Big E ride with me. I like the bus, I chill. If I want peace and quiet, that's where I get it—not that I want it too often.

The Star Bus is like my home-away-from-home. It's got a kitchen area in the front, with a microwave and a grill for making hamburgers. Of course, none of us cooks. If we're desperate, we'll do canned soups. We've got six bunk beds in the middle section of the bus, stacked up three high on each side. The back of the bus is *my* private quarters. I've got a big bed back there, a bathroom with a shower, lots of closet space— I've got lots of clothes, real luxurious, and all mine!

The bus has two TV sets and a VCR, so we can keep up with all the movies on tape if we want to, a slammin' stereo system, and—couldn't live without it—a Nintendo system. If I'm not sleeping, you'll find me playing Nintendo.

I am the Technobowl champ, chump! No one can touch me on that, I dare anyone to try! It's my specialty, I play it all the time. Earthquake plays with me sometimes. E-Rock used to be my number one challenger, but he's not on this tour. I get so into it, I don't want to stop even when we've gotten to our destination. You can hear me yellin' from the back of the bus, "Don't turn the generator off, I'm in the middle of a game!"

Another video game I play all the time on the bus is Gameboy, a hand-held Nintendo thing for one person usually. John Bush likes to play dominos on the bus—'cause that's what he can win at!—so we do that, too. We play different variations. John's favorite is "Hot Seat 101," where if you lose you're eliminated. It's cool, it's fun sometimes.

John doesn't usually have that much time to play, though. He's got to be on the phone—yeah, we got one in the bus—doing the advance work for me, that is, checking if things are cool in the city we're heading towards. Plus, he's got to keep an eye on me—not an easy job!

A TYPICAL CRAZY DAY

Once we get where we're going, it's hotel check-in time. I like nice hotels with big, comfortable rooms. I mean, we've been in some dives, with rooms the size of matchboxes. That is definitely *not* cool with me. It may sound spoiled, but I do a lot of work in those hotel rooms—and I bring a lot of stuff with me.

I always travel with my boom box. It's really dope—it's got a remote control. I always travel with a bunch of tapes, Big Daddy Kane, Eric B. & Rakim, and Audio II.

Being on the road so much, I have to listen to my own remixes on my boom box, too. So there's always a few of them lying around the hotel rooms. In fact, there's always Vanilla Ice paraphernalia around. Last time I carried the four-foot high *To The Extreme* cut-out with me wherever I went, and I always have tapes of myself doin' TV appearances around. People give me this stuff and it *is* meaningful to me. I'm not at the point yet where I'm jaded about anything. It's *all* still a kick and a half.

One thing about hotel rooms, we *never* trash 'em. Vanilla Ice is not into that scene. You hear about rock stars trashin' hotel rooms, having parties and stuff. We may be wild, and we certainly are *loud*—we've got the music cranked up all the time and the TV always going in the background—but we don't do damage. In fact, I'm pretty neat. Guess it's my mother's influence. If you come into my room, any hotel, any city, you'll be surprised. I pick up after myself. I don't order room service, either, so there's never any of that half-eaten garbage lying around. When I'm out on the road I'd much rather go out for pizza.

I eat a lot of pizza, pasta and junk food on the road, won't deny it. Snapple Iced Tea is my drink of choice. I drink it *all the time*, by the bottle, man—nothing else, nothing harder. I don't drink beer and I don't drink liquor. I never got into the habit, and I am not starting now. I see other rock and rap acts on the road—we run into people all the time—that are smashed, especially late at night. It's not my trip, makes me sick to see it.

I take vitamins on the road, but I don't exercise or work out, other than dancing. I dance every single day, and that's a serious, serious workout, not just on stage, but we rehearse on the road, too. Sometimes we rehearse for two to four hours a day.

When we get a chance, me and the posse like to shoot hoops if we can find a basketball court somewhere. There's not too much "down" time on the road, and I'm not much for reading, but I never miss an issue of Billboard. That's the music industry magazine that shows how your records are doing on the charts. I follow that one religiously—word!

But the truth is, we don't have time for a whole lot of anything. When we're out, we're out for a reason. Even though we might be doing a show at night, our days are filled. There's always stuff to do. There's always interviews to do. Sometimes I feel like I've done a million—realistically, it could be 20 a day.

The ones I like best are the radio interviews. I can do them on the phone from the hotel room, so I don't have to go anywhere. And radio deejays, they're the guys spinning my records, so I'm always grateful to them and happy to do whatever they ask. I don't forget who helped me when I was struggling—I never forget to say "thank you." So now that I'm big, when a radio station asks me to do an on-air interview, or just a quick promo message, I always say "Cool." And I do it.

I make up little four-line raps for the stations, change each one according to the call letters of the station or the deejay's name. All they have to do is give me a few key letters or names and I bust a rhyme on the spot, live on the phone for them. Give you an example. Here's what I usually start with:

> "Yo! This is Vanilla Ice,
> Chillin' like Bob Dylan,
> And maxin' like Michael Jackson,
> And livin' like Thanksgivin'."

Then, I might say something like:

> "Yo! This is Vanilla Ice,
> Kickin' it colder than ever,
> Playin' that funky music
> With Scramblin' Sam,
> on WOWE, babee!"

I got a million variations:

> "Here comes the perfect 10 at 10,
> (if the station is doing a Top 10 countdown)
> Bust it my friend!
> Kickin' it colder than ever,
> 'Cause Vanilla Ice is really clever."

I could do radio rhymes all day long, don't mind 'em at all. But there's other press I do on the road. Some of them come right to the hotel room, some bring video cameras, all that stuff. So I've got to look good and sound good all day long.

To give you a real clear idea of what a week on the road with Vanilla Ice is like, here's a crazy one we had not too long ago.

We started in Toronto, Canada, on a Monday. We began to shoot the "Stop That Train" video, and finished it the next morning, Tuesday. Then Tuesday night we did a concert on the Hammer tour. Wednesday morning I went into a studio in Montreal with Earthquake to cut the Ninja Rap song we wrote for the movie I'm in, *Teenage Mutant Ninja Turtles II*. Then Wednesday night, I did another Hammer show. Thursday, we flew down to New Orleans where I had two club dates to play, and Friday we went up and played Cleveland, Ohio, on the Hammer tour. Right after Cleveland, we hopped a Lear jet to Huntington, West Virginia, and played another show that same night—I was headlining—and the next day, we went to Carbondale, Illinois! In between all this stuff, there were interviews, rehearsals, a million phone calls— you name it, we did it.

Understand now where this line comes from: "I don't have no time, all I got time for is to bust a rhyme!"?

A BACKSTAGE PASS

The first time I set foot at a venue is to do the soundcheck, which is a little pre-concert ritual all performers do. We usually go over the afternoon before the show and see where all our stuff is being set up, making sure everything works so there are no surprises when we get out onstage that night.

During soundcheck is the first time I get really

pumped for that night's show—to look at me, you'd hardly know there was no audience there. I start movin', dancin', changing things around. My posse knows you got to be flexible to work with Ice. You ask them whether or not I make 'em crazy changing routines around at the soundchecks. I'm always movin' and improvin'. Knowing I'm going *on* soon, that's all it takes to get me pumped and the creative juices flowing.

It's really good that we have that time, too, because when we're backstage at night, just before we go on, there's no time to work on the music or anything. Soon as we get there, there are people waiting for us— waiting for me.

There's always press people to deal with backstage, journalists from magazines and newspapers, representatives from the record company, sometimes people from the promoter's office, too.

What I like best, though, is the time set aside backstage for the nightly "Meet & Greet." That's when I get to go face-to-face with the fans. I meet radio station contest winners, plus any and all fans who've gotten hold of a backstage pass somehow. I talk to *all* of them, I pose for pictures with every single one, I autograph anything. I love my fans, man. I appreciate them and I don't say no. A lot of the younger kids bring gifts for me, trinkets, teddy bears. The girls bring roses, and that's a real sweet thing to do, though it isn't necessary.

We hardly ever turn down a special request. Lots of times we'll be asked to allow handicapped kids backstage and for me, it's a privilege to meet *them*. Yo, if I can bring a little sunshine into their lives, that's a trip all by itself. When it comes to that stuff, if we can help somebody, some organization, if we can *possibly* do it, we will. We just say "yes."

After the "Meet & Greet," I usually head back to the dressing room and deal with stuff like makeup, hair and wardrobe. What trips people out is that I do it myself. Usually, you've got professional makeup people and hair stylists hired to do that for the performer. But *this* performer doesn't want that kind of help. I do it myself. Truth is, even for the stage, I don't need much makeup, just some powder to absorb the sweat. My hair's usually fine before I get to the show—the only thing I need to do backstage is add more hairspray. I go through a lot of *that* stuff!

I have different stage outfits I like to wear. I'm into a lot of black, white and silver—real shiny stuff.

The closer it gets to the time I go on, the more pumped I get—anyone around me can tell. I start doing headrolls and all sorts of gyrations. I'm poppin' and nothing can keep me still. It's not nervous energy— well, maybe it is. I do still get the butterflies before I go on, but they don't last long. Mainly, I am seriously juiced to get out there and kick it!

The last thing I do before we go out, though, is the thing that centers me. Everyone who's there backstage with me, the posse, whoever else is in the room, we all join hands in one big circle and say a prayer. We thank God for each day and ask Him to be with us at this performance. I feel, we all feel, that God got us here, and we can't abandon prayer now. It's especially important now, at the moment before we hit the stage.

WORKIN' IT ONSTAGE!

This is what it's all about. The platinum records, the money, the fame, the gold jewelry, none of it means anything without the performing. The fun part is going out and getting to do what got you here. The concerts are for me now what the street fights and motocross and rap competitions were for me all the time I was growing up. Ice grooves on competition, on challenge—especially in front of an audience—and that's what I got now when I do a show. Rockin' the crowd, that's what I live for. Bottom line: I *love* it.

If I had butterflies before, they're gone by the time I take my first step. It's real hard to get nervous when you know people are going to like you. I know that sounds big-headed, but we are very secure out there. We've got to be secure. We've got to know the crowd is going to go crazy for us out there, because they have every single time before. We're at the point on-stage where we know exactly how the crowd's going to react if we do something. So I'm just pumped—it is so much fun!

As I've said, I choreograph every single move you see on stage, for myself and the dancers, too. And I never lip sync, at least not when I have a choice. I hate lip syncing, but sometimes, if you're doing a TV show, you don't have that choice. I'm at the point in my career now where I can stay away from those kinds of situations. I can just turn them down.

Every show is dope, but some naturally have been more memorable than others: like the time when this girl in the front row pulled her shirt up, took off her bra and threw it up onstage. I mean, usually the lights are so bright you can hardly see the audience, but, word! I saw *that* one! I mean, I ran over there and just looked, thinking, "Oh my God, this is nuts!!" So what could I do? I picked up the bra and put it over my head. So the whole crowd laughed so hard, they were just rollin' about this, man. That was just hilarious.

And then there was the time on the Hammer tour when we totally messed up onstage. It happened this one time in Albuquerque, New Mexico. I mean, nobody knew it except us, but we messed up real bad. The drum machine wouldn't load, the DAT—digital audio tape—had fast-forwarded. See, the DAT player goes really fast, and it had fast-forwarded by itself and made this whooshing sound. When that happens, there's no way you can go back to the same spot you were at. You can't rewind it, 'cause then the crowd would really know you messed up.

'Quake hit the drum machine and we just played it off. He was going, "Oh, no," and I was just ad-libbing, talking to the crowd for the longest time, it seemed. See, there was a drum machine, but no music, so we couldn't even dance. It was so funny, looking back on it. I was just going to the crowd, "Huh! Everybody say, 'Ho-o-o-h!,' say, 'Ho-o-o-h!' " I even had to go into our old stuff because I didn't know what to say, and you can't just say nothing and leave it all quiet.

To myself I was thinking, " 'Quake, please, *please* give me some music, give me *something!*" Nobody in the audience realized what was going on, and finally—seemed like forever!—'Quake got the music in and it came on.

The crowd loved it. I mean, they didn't know we messed up, they thought it was something we put in on purpose. And what really tripped us out, Hammer's people came by after the show and said, "You changed the show a little bit tonight, looks good!" Huh! They said it looked good!

AFTER THE SHOW

We are so pumped after each show that even though it's late, there's no chance of anyone wanting to go to bed. What we'd like to do is party, go to a dance club or something, but that kind of thing just gets harder and harder to do. You never know what the situation's going to be. I might get recognized and mobbed and that would take the fun out of it. So we usually just avoid it and go out and grab some food.

We are always hungry and always in search of someplace open late-night for a bite. No matter what we do, we always hang together. When we're on the road, the posse—including John Bush—is together, 24–7. We're together so much we can read each other's minds, which we do.

ICE INTERNATIONAL

Europe was a trip of another kind. Since the record got released there, it's been pandemonium. We had to go. Naturally, I had never been there—where would a street kid from Miami get the money to go to Europe?—so it was a big deal the first time.

We flew the Concorde there. What a trip, man! Smooth as Ice's rhymes, goin' the speed of sound at 53,000 feet above. Three and a half hours later we're in London. Everybody there calls me "Vernilla Eyes," but the fans, man, were really trippin'. They were outside the hotel all day and all night long, mobbing me wherever I went. Thankfully, the security was great, because when those fans get a hold of you, they can do some major damage—take some body parts!

A few did get to me and tore some of my gold chains off, but I recovered them. I hate to think of what these kids are like when they're mad! We had to call 40 policeman out when I did a live TV show called *Wogan* in London. It's like the *Tonight Show* here, usually pretty stodgy, but when I went on, I kicked that thing alive, man!

Gotta admit, the first time I went to Europe—I've been there twice now—I didn't really like it. I don't like going into restaurants where I couldn't read the menu! Forget foreign food—I'm from the streets, man, and I could not adapt to it at all.

The second time I went over, which was just a couple of months later, I liked everything better. Couldn't do much sight-seeing, which was too bad. I did a *lot* of press there, a lot of magazines, newspapers and photo shoots. I also did a record signing at a store, and there was a line around the block.

I did other TV shows there, like *Smash Hits* and *Top of the Pops*. In Munich, Germany, the reaction of the fans was the same, even though they don't speak English. They seemed to understand every word I said. It's slammin'!

Right after I went there, the kids in both cities made me Number One. "Ice Ice Baby" went number one on the charts in England and Germany. They honored me with a gold plaque; *that* was slammin'!

MELTING ICE

12

*"And I'll never forget
what you mean to me,
Comin' straight from the heart
of Vanilla I-C-E."*

SO FAR IN this book, I've been telling you the truth about myself, and how we kicked off the Ice boom. Like that old soul song says, "If you don't know me by now, you will never ever know me at all . . ." But if you've gotten this far and still don't have a handle on the *real* Ice man, I'll use this chapter for some melt-down. Maybe show you another side of myself. Cool?

You'll probably never hear me admit this stuff again, so listen up!

THE REAL VANILLA ICE BELIEVES IN . . .

LOYALTY

That's a high priority. It's like I've said before, I'll never forget where I came from. Well, I'll never forget the people who started with me, stuck with me and got me here, either. I hope I never change in that way, become one of those phonies who ditches "all the little people" soon as he's on top. That's not my scene. That's not *Ice*. Just about everyone who started with me is still with me. There were a few who dropped out on their own accord, like E-Rock. But not many. The people who struggled with me, Tommy, John Bush and Earthquake are here for the big payoff.

Give you another example. The radio station KMEL in San Francisco was real helpful in convincing Hammer's people to take us on the tour. After that, I broke through the roof. But when they asked me to come and give a New Year's Eve concert there, I said, "Absolutely." I mean, with the popularity I have now, I could've been in Japan, or doing something really major. I didn't *have* to go to San Francisco for a radio gig. But hey, man, they helped me. If my being there can help them, I'm there.

PATRIOTISM

We're real lucky to live in this country, and that's something I don't forget. Sure, the U.S.A. has problems, but it's still the only place in the world where anyone can make it, no matter where you come from. It's like I always say: It's not where you come from, it's where you're at that counts.

If you have a dream and work really hard, you can make it. I made it—a kid from the streets, no money, no higher education, no powerful family behind me. No one bought and paid for Vanilla Ice. I had a talent, I had a dream; I worked hard, was lucky enough to hook up with good people, and I made it. That couldn't have happened—at least not so fast—in any other country in the world. I know that's true.

EQUALITY

To me, everyone's the same, and I'm not just talking about skin color. I look at people as just people, no one more important than the other, no matter what they do—whether they're a doctor, teacher, President of the United States or rapper. I don't get intimidated by people with fancy titles, or people with money or power. I'm a good judge of people, and I can tell right off what kind of person someone is—I trust my own judgment, and I haven't been wrong yet.

HONESTY

If you haven't noticed by now, I say exactly what's on my mind. Ice doesn't fake it—I'm not a hypocrite. If I don't like something, I say it. It might sound harsh, but if it's how I really feel, I'd rather you know about it. I keep no secrets from the people around me, and they're honest with me, too.

ABSOLUTES

I'm not wishy-washy about anything, especially about my relationships with people. It goes along with being loyal. If I love you, I always will, no matter what. But if you mess with me even once, if you betray me, I'll have nothing to do with you forever. That's how I am. I'm not saying that's a great way to be, but it is the way I am. And like I said, I'm nothin' if not honest.

GOD

I know I've said it before, it's kind of a theme in this book, but that's only because my belief in God is so strong. I believe in myself, too. But in the end, God is what got me here. God put Vanilla Ice right here.

I pray every day and, since I started, look what's happened for me. I never had anything great like this happen to me before. And that's the way I'd like to go down. Because of God, I feel that now I can truly be a role model for kids out there who want to look up to me. I feel comfortable about that now.

And I rely on God to remind me that I may be a star, but I can't ever think I'm bigger than Him. What goes up must come down. Belief in God keeps me humble.

THE REAL VANILLA ICE IS . . .

STILL A KID AT HEART

If you chip away at the Ice—get to know me real well—you'll see that in lots of ways I'm still a kid. Having all this happen to me still feels a lot like that Christmas when I woke up and saw that big box under the tree with my motorcycle outfit in it. I get excited—maybe overexcited—very easily. That comes across as boasting to some people, I understand that, but I'm still trippin' out about this whole scene, and I'm still easily impressed by a lot of it.

Which is not to say I haven't learned a lot about the hard realities of this business. I'm learning something new every day. I'm learning about the music, about money, about banks, investments, real estate, the busi-

ness end of it all. But I'm not jaded yet. Maybe someday, but not yet.

I'm impulsive, I laugh easily—*anything* makes me
laugh, other people, funny things. I've got a great
sense of humor. Kids make me laugh. I love kids. I
love to get down on the floor and play with little kids. I
have a real feel for them—probably because I *am* one!

CONFIDENT & COCKY, BUT NOT (TOO) COLD

I have a strong personality. I have a hot temper—
I've even been called "The Sean Penn of Rap," even
though I never knocked out a photographer. I am confident, I have to be. It's part of rap and it's part of
what got me here. If you don't believe you're number
one, no one else is going to either. So I don't apologize
for that attitude coming through.

But there is another side to my personality. I don't
believe in being rude to people, even if they provoke
me. I really *try* to keep it cool. I feel weird having to
say this about myself, but underneath it all, I am a
nice guy. I'm a good guy, anyone that really knows
me will tell you. I can be the nicest guy in the world.
That's why people put up with the other side of me,
I guess.

NEVER DOES DRUGS

That's no hype, no image thing. I was around it,
I've seen it. I know lots of people that were into it,
close, close friends that sold drugs, but I never had
anything to do with it. Partly, as I told you, it was
because of the motocross that I had to stay healthy and
in top athletic shape. I couldn't have any of that stuff

in my system. But I also had the attitude growing up, and still have it now, that, bottom line: I'm not gonna ruin my life. Even if I'm exposed to it every day, I'm not gonna mess with it. I care more about myself than I do about getting involved with drugs.

NEVER CRIES

I don't cry and I don't know why. No amount of pain has made me cry. I've been through the worst physical pain you can imagine—I've screamed, but never cried. When I was a little kid, I didn't cry either. I've always solved my own problems without crying for help.

The closest I ever came to crying was not when I was a kid, but recently. My eyes got real watery the night in New York when the record company people presented me with platinum record plaques. I had the number one record in the country that week, but I didn't know they were going to surprise me with a presentation. Right then and there is when I lived my dream come true—actually lived it. That's when I realized I'm off the streets for the rest of my life. That's when it hit me. I got it made. I just went "boom!" It all hit me right there. My eyes got watery, but luckily I had some makeup on my face from performing earlier that night, so nobody could really tell. To them, it looked like I was smiling. But it's as close to crying as I've ever come.

MORE THINGS ABOUT ME...

I AM A SPORTS FANATIC—especially about Miami, my hometown teams. I don't get to go to many games, but I catch 'em when I can. The Dolphins' defense is slammin'. Marino is the best quarterback there is and Shula is the best coach. They deserve the Super Bowl. Word! I love the Heat, I love the Hurricanes—I'm behind them all the way.

I LISTEN TO all rap music and lots of reggae, too. I like Yellowman, UB40, Bob Marley and Ziggy Marley.

I GO TO THE MOVIES rarely, but I love going. I think Charlie Sheen's a great actor. I like all his movies. I met him in Los Angeles and it turns out that he's a big Vanilla Ice fan. So that's really cool. When I'm in L.A., we get together and we kick it.

I DON'T WATCH TV, at least not in terms of sitting down to a particular show. I just don't have time. When I did, I used to like *21 Jump Street*. They even used "Ice Ice Baby" in one of their episodes. I do watch a show if I've been on it, of course, like *The Rick Dees Show* or *MTV*. And if I'm in a hotel room or something, the TV is always on in the background. That's how I catch the news.

I LOVE TO PARTY, especially with my homeys, my good friends. My idea of a great party is staying up all night, listening to music, dancing, with everyone having a good time and *no fighting*.

WHAT I'VE LEARNED ABOUT MONEY

Until last year, I never had any money, never had a dime. Now I've got more than I ever dreamed of. It's funny, because when you dream about having a

lot of money, you think it's gonna be a certain way—
your life is gonna change and everything's gonna be
perfect. At least that's how I used to feel.

What I've learned is that in some ways, having
money is everything it's cracked up to be—but like
the old cliche says, it can't buy everything. Having
money has changed my lifestyle, but it hasn't changed
my life.

I've splurged on gold jewelry. That's something I've
always wanted, but could never afford. I used to think
that even if I could afford it, I'd never spend an out-
rageous amount on one piece of jewelry. But this one
ring looked so good that I did. I bought a gold and
diamond ring that's huge, really slammin'. I bought
chains, watches, bracelets and other rings—all rappers
wear gold jewelry.

I bought a car, an expensive Acura NSX—which
is the Playboy Car of the Year. It's a two-seater and
all-white, inside and out.

I bought toys: a remote-control, four-wheel-drive
truck and a remote-control airplane. I crashed it the
first time I flew it, so I named it "Crash." See what
I meant about part of me still being a kid at heart?

Having money has allowed me to buy two homes,
one for my mother and one for myself. I was proud
to be able to do that, 'cause my mother has been in
the same house *forever*. And it was real good to be
able to move her.

Even better was being able to give her a gift I know
she's always dreamed of—a baby grand piano. In fact,
thinking about the day I gave it to her makes me realize
that there were two times I came close to tears. My
eyes got all watery, 'cause I felt like finally I'm able
to give her something back, something that's tangible

and real. I wanted to say, "Mom, you've done so much for me, and I know I put you through hell. Here's a small token of my appreciation," but the words didn't come. I think she understood, though.

There's a lot that money can't buy, and the one that's hit me hardest is *time*. Money can't buy time. This *is* my time, my time to shine, but because of that, I have no time, no time for myself anymore. And I miss that.

WHEN I GET HOME

Being on the road so much, I don't get home very often. So I spend a lot of time dreaming about what I'm going to do when I get there.

Home *now* is Dallas, I will admit that. I bought a house there, my car is there and, when I'm home, my favorite thing to do is drive it! I've driven it a total of two and a half days since I've had it, and for someone who loves cars and speed so much, that's a bummer. So when I get home, I head for my car *first!*

I've got a new hobby now, jet-skiing. My friend got me into it. We go out on a lake near Dallas. It's like motorcycling on water. If you crash, you hit water instead of asphalt or dirt, so it's a little safer than motocross. I used to borrow my friend's skis, but now that I have money, I bought my own. Of course now that I have my own, I have no time to use them.

The best part about being home is getting to see my friends and family, hanging out with Darron "The Squirrel" Wehland and all my family. Lately, I don't see them enough. So when I *am* with them, I just appreciate it and make the most of it.

ICE ON...
MY GIRLS,
MY STYLE
& MY FANS

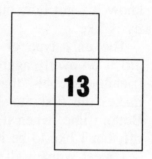

13

"Ladies, I wanna rock with you..."

A LOT OF my raps have to do with girls, which makes sense because I am *very* interested in the ladies. I started early, by kindergarten I had my first girlfriend. I always had girlfriends, I was always very popular, always a ladies man. When I was a teenager, girls became something else to compete about—my friends and I would see who could get a certain girl to like him first.

I love all women—all sizes, all shapes, all personalities. The only things that turn me off about a woman is if she smokes, drinks alcohol or takes drugs. Smoking is the worst. I *hate* cigarettes. I have never smoked, no one in the posse smokes. The smell of it makes me choke.

I go for clean-cut girls. Of course, the first thing I notice about a girl is her looks. I can't lie about it. My first impression of a girl, whether I'm going to be drawn to her or not, is based on her looks. I know it's not fair, but then I see what her personality is like.

The only type of personality I can't stand in a girl is an overly aggressive one. Being outgoing and friendly is cool—that's good, I like it when a girl makes the first move—but too much is *too much*. Bottom line, when it comes to girls, she can kick it off, but I like to be in control—right from the start.

I meet women all over, at clubs, on the road, in restaurants, backstage at concerts, driving in my car, every place. 'Cause I'm *always* looking. If a girl is looking for me, the best way to get my attention is to dress super-sexy and then, when you meet me, play me like you don't know who I am. Talk to me like I'm just any guy you're attracted to. Because my one big problem with the ladies now that I didn't have *before* I got famous is not knowing who's interested in *me* and who just wants to say she hung out with a celebrity. It's hard for me to tell, which is a drag.

I like girls who are real romantic, because I'm the king of the romance scene, baby. When I'm with a girl, I'm Mr. Charm, her very own personal "lucky charm." I'm the man, the man with the plan! It's like I wrote: "Ladies, I wanna rock with you, and later in the night y'know, I'd like to pursue, Something real smooth and nice, That's why they call me Vanilla Ice, yep, yep!"

My idea of a romantic date is cruisin' in my car

with a special lady, rolling the windows up so we're real cozy, and throwing a Ready For The World tape on, the one with that song that goes, "Let me love you down..." I'd be singing along with the tape, singing just to her. Then we'd go someplace for dinner, but it would have to be a secluded place, not somewhere that I'd be recognized. I like candlelit romantic restaurants, but not those where the menu is so fancy that I don't know what I'm ordering. I don't mind spending a lot of money when I take a girl out to dinner, but I can't get into those foreign-sounding delicacies.

So a real elegant restaurant is fine, as long as I can get stuff I'm familiar with. Truth is, I'm happiest with a place where I can get hamburgers, cheeseburgers and chicken wings. I do like lobster and lobster tails. The perfect restaurant, now that I think of it, is the Rusty Pelican in Miami, right on Key Biscayne. Yeah, that would be a perfect place to take a girl.

After that, if I was in Miami, I'd take a moonlit walk on the boardwalk, or by a lake or river or something. I like being by the water, walking hand-in-hand, just talking. That's what I mean by romantic.

I have never been really hooked on a woman, not the way E-Rock is, anyway. I have had two serious, long-term relationships. The last one ended pretty recently. It was real heavy. I was with her for three years. I had real serious thoughts about her, thinking maybe that she's the one I might marry someday. I cared about her a lot.

But in the end, she wanted to get married. She wanted me to quit my career, settle down in Dallas with her and get married. She gave me a choice—

either her or Vanilla Ice. I was out the door that second. I have the rest of my life to get married. I don't have the rest of my life to be Vanilla Ice. So it wasn't much of a choice, really. But that's why it ended.

Right now, I have no serious girlfriend at all. I'm on the road so much, it's impossible. I meet girls every night of the week! Sometimes I get lonely. I do miss the relationship thing, but right now in my career, it's more important to be on the road. There *are* a bunch of girls in Dallas who think they're Vanilla Ice's girl, but—I hope this doesn't get me in trouble—there's no *one* special girl. There's also no one I'm really dying to meet—except maybe Janet Jackson, 'cause she's so fine!

THE ICE STYLE

People come up to me all the time and tell me I look like the football player Jim McMahon, or movie legend James Dean. I've read where I look like Billy Idol, too. I don't agree with any of that. I am 100 percent original. I don't follow trends—I set them.

I've had lots of looks over the years, lots of hairstyles. Like the one I have now—the beak with a streak and the lines on the sides and in the back—I created them all myself. I started that one in high school, as I told you.

But what really trips people out is not only that I created my hairstyles, but that I cut my own hair and style my own hair—do the zigzag lines, arrows, stripes all by myself. I sit where there's a mirror behind me and hold another mirror in front of me. That way I can see my whole head. I use electric clippers to draw the lines. I keep changing the designs, too. I've written "Ice" in the back of my hair, I've written "Miami," I've had "Vanilla" and every single different design you can think of. Just recently, I started to do lines in my left eyebrow. Everyone else was putting lines in their hair, so naturally I had to do something different!

To get my hair real high in the front, where the streak is, I use mousse and hairspray—a *lot* of hairspray. But not just any hairspray, I've got this one special kind I use. When I travel, I've got one suitcase just for my hairsprays and mousses. I'm proud of the way my hair looks and I'll tell you a secret. I don't like to be photographed unless my hair is perfect— that's why you'll see pictures of me in baseball caps a lot. If I don't think my hair's right, and I'm in a hurry, I'd rather slap a baseball cap on than have people see my hair messed.

I don't have any facial hair, but I used to have a goatee, a serious, good-looking goatee. It didn't really go with the Vanilla Ice image, plus I found that the girls didn't really dig it, so I shaved it off.

I'm a serious clothes freak. I love clothes, and I have closets full at home. It's not because of any image thing, I was always into clothes, even before I could afford anything really nice and hip. My style hasn't really changed, I still like to wear stuff that's different and colorful. I like to look good and, as always, I like to stand out—offstage as well as on.

I do wear some designer-type jeans and shirts, now that I can afford them. I always wear sneakers and funky shades. I buy all my underwear at Victoria's Secret. I've been buying it there for years. A lot of people think that store only has fancy ladies' lingerie, but they've got great men's underwear, too.

Lately, I've been wearing checked or striped patterned Skidz overalls, unhooked to the waist. Practically all my T-shirts or sweatshirts say something about Miami on them—sometimes, it's just the name of the city, others are team shirts from the Dolphins, Heat or Hurricanes. I've got a whole bunch of sweats from the University of Miami. Nothin' against Dallas, but Miami *is* my hometown, and I'm proud to advertise that.

Of everything I own, my new denim jacket is my favorite. It was a gift from my record company. They took me on a tour of New York a few months back, and we stopped in a little shop in Soho. I picked out a denim jacket, and they had the word "ICE" airbrushed on the back and on the sleeves—too cool, man.

Speaking of gifts from the record company, another thing they gave me is my big "Number One" gold pendant that I wear around my neck. That's really slammin', because, yo! I'm a rapper and most rappers do wear gold. At any given time, I usually wear at least two gold chains, five rings, my brand-new Gucci watch, a couple of earrings and a bracelet.

ICE FAN-TASIES

None of this would be possible without the fans, and I'm the first one to acknowledge that. No matter how good I am, or how smart my manager is, or even how strong my faith is, if the fans don't like my music, I'm back on the car lot in Dallas. Just the thought of having fans trips me out! All the time I was trying to make it, I never really thought about that aspect of it. It's part of the whole dream-come-true.

I get over 2,000 pieces of fan mail a day. I do read some of it, but I won't lie: The truth is, I'm on the road so much, I really don't get to read many letters individually. I do see to it that everyone who writes gets something back, an acknowledgment, at least. We set up a fan club so anyone who wants to can get posters and pictures and the latest news about my career. The address is: The Vanilla Ice Fan Club, P.O. Box 261117, Plano, TX 75026-1117. Even if I can't say thank you personally to everyone who writes, I do *care*, and I would like to show it any way I can. I don't take *any* of it for granted.

I do have some messages for my fans. For the ones that might be growing up like me—poor, on the streets—don't do what I did. Don't give in to peer pressure and get into bad things. Don't mess your body up, don't get in with the gangs. Try and find one friend, someone who thinks like you do, and stick with him or her. Don't worry about what everyone else thinks or says. Stay in school even if you think you're not learning anything. You never know what's in the future. Don't close any doors for yourself before you've even started. Do the right thing, you know in your heart what that is.

If you want to be a rapper, or whatever you want to be, know that you can do it. Have a goal and go for it. Be determined and don't let anything stop you. If I made it, so can you.

In my heart, I live for my fans. When I'm up onstage is when I like to think I show it. When I'm performing, I don't just give 100 percent, I give 1,000 percent. And when they're clapping and cheering for me, inside

I'm cheering for *them*—and saying "thank you" every single second, "thank you so much for making this possible, for making my dream come true." I hope I can keep on paying you guys back by doing my best. I sure as hell am going to try.

THE (PR)ICE
OF FAME

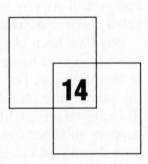

14

"Don't believe the hype,
'cause that's not right ..."

BYRON HAS A saying: "Life will pay you and life will charge you." I never knew what that meant until last year when I became famous. I've been paid in ways I never dreamed possible, but I've had to pay in others that are just as unbelievable. It's been one wild rollercoaster ride, yep, yep!

There's a lot of great things about being famous, no denying that. For a kid who always wanted to be in the spotlight, well, this is the ultimate spotlight, man. I get to do what I love doing best, and for it, I get huge amounts of money, recognition, respect and the power to be creatively in control of my music. Selling over seven million records in the United States alone validates my talent and the direction we've chosen for Vanilla Ice.

I get a kick out of being famous. I still get a thrill when I hear my songs on the radio, or see one of my

145

videos on TV. I can't get enough of watching them. I tape every TV appearance I've done and watch those over and over too. It's exciting to see yourself on TV—it's *fun*, man!

Kids looking up to me, asking for my autograph, coming to the concerts and buying the records—all that is still trippin' me out, and I hope I never get jaded about that. That is how life has paid me.

But I've been charged plenty. There's more than one bad side to being famous and I've faced them all in the past year. For one thing, fame has taken away my private life. It's killed my private life, shattered it. I *have* no private life anymore. They say that's what happens to superstars, and they say that's what I am now. I can't go out in public without security around me constantly. I can't go to parties with my friends. I can't go to clubs or restaurants where I might be mobbed.

Being famous means having no time for myself, because I've made all these commitments—hell, I'm committed up through 1992. I don't have a spare moment until 1992, imagine what that's like. But I've learned enough about the business to know that if I start turning things down, if I try to get out of these bookings, concerts and appearances, that's the beginning of the end for Vanilla Ice. That's the downfall of Vanilla Ice.

Fame brings pressure, man, pressure to stay on top. Just as I took the number one spot from M.C. Hammer, no doubt someone's gonna take it from me. And that's cool, I wish the next guy the best. But I've got to keep working, keep trying to get it back, keep coming up with new and better material. Being on top means there's only one direction you can go—and I'm gonna fight *not* to go in that direction.

People come out of the woodwork when you're famous. Suddenly all these people consider me their old pal and make statements to the press like, "Oh, yeah, I knew him, I was his best friend." Wrong! I hardly knew these people at all! This one guy said he was my roommate—he slept over my house one night because he didn't have a ride home! Does that make him my roommate? And this girl who said she knew me real well in high school in Carollton—I never heard of her. Besides, *no one* knew me real well in high school. I wasn't in any one high school long enough for anyone to know me. And as I told you, the kids in school had no idea what I was doing on the weekends in South Dallas. They didn't know *any* of it. But now that I'm famous, I guess they feel it's a good way to get their names in the paper. So whether it's true or not, they're coming out with it.

My personal life getting messed with *is* the real downside of being famous—and that's directly related to the press, to what newspapers and magazines print about me. I'm not denying that their writing about me *has* helped my career. There are some people that think it doesn't matter *what* they say about you, as long as your name's in the paper. I guess a part of me feels that way.

When I took my pants off to prove I was stabbed—more about that in a sec—I know that the girls all talked about the red underwear I had on, and something like that's gonna be talked about more than whether I lied or not. I understand that and it's kind of funny. But when there's more in the press about my personal background than about my music, I wonder if the benefits are outweighing the invasion of privacy.

As everyone knows by now, I've had a lot of problems with the press—a *lot* of problems. People come to interview me, and in the beginning it was all so new to me, I didn't turn anyone down. Whether I was bummed, or tired, or hungry or whatever—I never said "No" to an interview. And I was ready to answer all their questions, as best as I could—but hardly any of those interviews, except the radio ones, turned out the way I thought they would.

For one thing, right off the bat, they all seemed to have the same exact questions. They all wanted to talk about the same two things—the black/white thing and the censorship thing. I've already told you how I feel about the race thing. I wish it weren't an issue, that there was no racism in this country. Racism *makes* it an issue in the first place. As for censorship, it really hasn't been something I've faced, so I don't spend a lot of time thinking about it. I censor myself.

I don't curse in my raps—I don't *have* to curse to express myself. If there's something else in my raps besides cursing that's objectionable, we usually talk about it. If I agree that it could be interpreted negatively, I take it out. My stuff *is* played on the radio. I do listen to other groups who do curse, and who are going through a lot of problems because of it. 2 Live Crew is one of my favorite groups, personally. If I were a parent, maybe I'd feel differently. Parents should have some control over what their kids listen to—of course, there wasn't a parent in the world who could've controlled me when I was a kid, so it's hard to really say.

But my other real big problem with the press is that they come in to interview me, and already prejudge me before they even meet me or hear what I have to say. They look at me, a white boy rapping, and automatically go, "He's lying. He can't have grown up in the streets. He's stealing rap from the black kids, he's making all this up.'' They just don't see a white guy growing up the way I did.

So of course when they say that to me, I look at it as a challenge—which is the way I look at everything, as you probably can tell by now—a challenge to prove myself. I never should have to. I don't see any other performer having to prove himself publicly. But actually had to *demean* myself, had to pull my pants down on national TV to show my scars from when I got stabbed. Do you know how humiliating that is? I had to prove something I'm not even proud of. And then it comes across that I'm bragging about my background, which isn't true at all.

I'm lucky to be in the position I'm in and I *want* to use it for the good—I want to be a role model for kids out there with a dream, but what kind of role model goes around bragging about being stabbed and dropping out of school? I was forced to have to do that stuff, because when they prejudged me and accused me of lying, I had to refute it. I had to take what I saw as a challenge.

I wrote a short rap just a few weeks ago, thinking about the press. It goes like this:

"Yo, this is Vanilla Ice,
About the media and the papers,
Not doin' me right.
All I gotta say is,
Don't believe the hype,
'Cause that's not right.
Vanilla Ice tells the truth,
And that's no lie."

Well, this is as good a time as any to go into all the other stuff that's been printed about me and to tell you the truth. So, here goes.

THE MIAMI-DALLAS STORY

I claim Miami as my hometown. A story came out in a Dallas newspaper that said, "No, he's from Dallas. Not only that, he's from a middle-class section of Dallas."

If you've read this book this far you know that I *did* grow up most of my life in Miami which is why I claim it as my hometown. When I was a teenager we did move to Dallas, as I told you, because of Byron's job.

A lot of good things happened for me in Dallas— everything great that happened for Vanilla Ice happened in Dallas. The whole organization, the whole posse's from Dallas. I've always said that.

I do owe a lot to Dallas. I've always thought of it as my second home. I'll probably buy new homes in both cities. But my roots are in Miami. I learned everything I know about rap, dance and beat-boxing in the streets of Miami. And if it weren't for that background, who would know—or *care*—about Vanilla Ice right now?

THE LUTHER CAMPBELL
HIGH SCHOOL STORY

I'll admit it, I twisted things a little on this one. I didn't lie—we both went to a lot of different high schools; one *was* the same, but we weren't there at the same time—but when the record company bio came out making it look like we went to the same school at the same time, I didn't do anything to correct it. I knew it wasn't exactly accurate, but I didn't go out of my way to have it fixed.

At the time it was written, I never thought I'd get so famous that every little thing written about me would be scrutinized so closely. This was all so new to me, I was trying to crack into a tough business—I thought maybe this would draw a little more attention to me, to the music. It was a mistake to mislead people—I see that now.

THE MOTOCROSS STORY

I said I won three national championships in the sport of motocross and the press said, "Well, we checked with Honda and the American Motocross Association and they never heard of you." Yo, I wasn't ever *with* the American Motocross Association so there's a good reason why they never heard of me. But the AMA isn't the only organization that runs motocross competitions all over the U.S.A.

There's another one called The Grand National Championships and that's who I rode for. Six years of my life I rode on tracks all over—and I did win three different times. You've read the story here in this book, you've seen the pictures, so you know I'm telling the truth. Whether the GNC is not as *national* as the AMA, I never knew that. I didn't realize, and I'm still not even *sure*, whether one is regional and one is national. When I won, I thought it was national—after all, it's called the Grand *National* Championship. I had no reason to think otherwise, or to tell the press otherwise. I stick by my story.

THE SATISFACTION STORY

I told you that a rap version of the Rolling Stones' "Satisfaction" was on my *Hooked* album, but not on *To The Extreme* because SBK couldn't get legal permission to sample some guitar riffs from it. After *To The Extreme* went to number one, I had a meeting with record company people and we talked about trying again for my upcoming live album. We even talked about the possibility of me doing it live with Mick Jagger.

Now, at the time, nothing was ever set—I don't know if they'd even asked Mick yet—but I got so excited about it, I did say something on TV that this might happen, that Mick and I might be performing live. This is another example of my inexperience and one I'm sorry about. When I said it, I didn't know enough about the business to realize that just because you discuss something with your record company doesn't mean it's automatically going to happen. A lot of great ideas—and wishful thinking—are tossed around when you talk. And sometimes they *do* happen; everything *starts* because someone had an idea. Anyway, I should never have blurted out that it was going to happen, made me look like . . . what else? A liar, again. I am young, I am inexperienced. I am learning.

THE FEUD WITH M.C. HAMMER STORY

I said I "touched" him and that part was true. Even he can't deny that *To The Extreme* knocked his LP out of number one. He said, "U Can't Touch This," and I did. I also think I can out-dance him and that got into the press, and they made a big deal out of it. Bottom line: As I've said, I think M.C. Hammer is one of the greatest performers ever. I give him all the credit in the world. I learned a lot from him. I'm grateful for the opportunity to have been on his tour. He's a great guy, and I give him all the respect. In my opinion, we are not feuding. We have different styles and we both think we're the best. But that's part of rap—like I said, you've *got* to think *you're* the best. We both do, but that doesn't make a feud.

THE REAL NAME STORY

I saved this one for last, because it's the most painful and complicated one. It also gets to the heart of a lot of this stuff. My real name is Robert Van Winkle. Thanks to the press, everyone knows that by now. I didn't ever want it to come out, but I see how naive that was of me to think it wouldn't.

I had really good reasons for not wanting my name to come out—I still have them. I see it's impossible to protect my privacy, that's out the window, man— but I'm still trying. I'm still *fighting* as hard as I can to protect my family's privacy. If that involves being mysterious about who they are and where they live, so be it.

My family are real decent, hardworking people. They're the fabric of America. They never had money, they always just worked hard, worked every single day, and were grateful for what they got. They are not impressed with fame or celebrity— they don't want to live vicariously through me. You don't see my family popping up at my gigs, trying to get their picture in the paper. They don't care about that stuff, it doesn't mean anything to them.

It's not that they aren't proud of Vanilla Ice, but they're private people.

Family and God are what's important, not fame and fortune. I respect that, and when I see it being messed with, I go off the top. Byron and my brother are trying to run their businesses selling cars, and when I see people bothering them, just coming to ask for their autographs and ask about Vanilla Ice, it makes me crazy.

The hardest part of all this is my mother. I love her so much and yes, I am *very* protective of her. As soon as I got famous, people started messing with her, started to call up and ring the doorbell, wanted to know about Vanilla Ice. So I moved her. I had to move her out of the house she's been in forever and move her into a new one. I had to *buy* privacy for my mother. I have asked her not to give interviews about me, not to answer questions, this is true. I don't want her in the spotlight, because *she* doesn't want to be in the spotlight. She's not well and the truth is, I put her through enough. I'd like her to relax and enjoy the good stuff that's happening to Vanilla Ice now—and not have to deal with the crap.

There's another, deeper reason that I'm fighting to insure my mother's privacy. Because of my background, I can't *ever* disregard the possibility of something bad happening to her. And if something ever did happen, that would be the end. All of this, everything I've achieved would be garbage, would be meaningless. I would be devastated and it would be the end of everything.

This is how I feel about it and this is why I have misled the press on occasion. I feel I'm justified, no matter what anybody else thinks.

Bottom line: I'm incredibly happy about all the wonderful things that have happened for me. It's a dream come true—but the dream comes with a price. I think I'm paying it.

FUTURE ICE

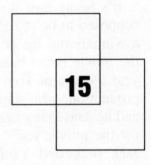

15

*"Believe me when I tell you,
I'm here to stay."*

I HAVE NEVER been afraid to take a risk. Just the opposite, I've lived for risks—and I don't have any intention of changing, not as a person and not as a performer. I've reached an incredible level of success so far, but I've got a lot farther to go. Here's a taste of what Ice will be serving up in the near future.

ICE ON SCREEN

The first time Tommy Quon saw me, he thought, "movie star." I don't know why he thought that—it wasn't something *I* ever thought. But movies are definitely in my future—in fact, I've already completed my first one.

It's called *Teenage Mutant Ninja Turtles II: The Secret Of The Green Ooze*. Yep, yep, it's the sequel to that blockbuster that took the country by storm. Like most young people who saw it, I loved it. I thought it was great. Never did I imagine I'd be asked to be in the sequel—that was slammin'! I won't say I star in it, 'cause the Turtles do, of course, but I have a cool role. I play myself—a rapper whose rhyming saves the day for Leonardo, Donatello, Raphael and Michaelangelo.

It's funny how it all came about, because I wasn't supposed to be in it. The part was actually written for a woman and the people who wrote it and produced the movie never heard of Vanilla Ice. It was the 12-year-old son of Tom Gray, the executive in charge of production, who suggested it. The kid's name is Jack and he said to his father, "Have you picked the music for the movie yet?" When his dad said they hadn't, Jack suggested Vanilla Ice, said all the kids at his school were hip to me. This was back in September.

So Tom Gray checked it out and found that I was with SBK and so are the Turtles music group, which made it easy for him to reach me. He called Charles Koppelman and asked about me—naturally Charles said I was about to be the hottest thing on the music scene.

Tom Gray and the Turtle people didn't waste any time. Their original idea was just to use my music for the movie, but after seeing the "Ice Ice Baby" video, they asked me if I'd like to actually appear in the movie. I didn't hesitate. I love movies and I love kids. Since *Teenage Mutant Ninja Turtles* is for kids, it was a perfect combination. Soon as I said "Yes," they got busy and wrote a scene for me to appear in. They call it a cameo. They asked if we could come to North Carolina at the end of October for filming. We were in the middle of the Hammer tour at that point, but luckily were able to get some time off to do it.

Making the movie was a real eye-opener. I had never

been on a movie set before and didn't know what to think. The first thing I learned is that movie making takes *forever*—it is *so* boring when you're just waiting around. And there's a lot of waiting around. Plus it was *hot* on that set, it was like a sauna, man, with steam and fog machines. Must've been 130 degrees. I really felt bad for the actors inside those Turtle suits! But those costumes are awesome, man! I was impressed. Word!

I didn't really do any *acting*, because there wasn't time. I had eight days to complete everything. My big scene was filmed on a soundstage set up to resemble a smoky basement called The Dockshore Club. I was up there rapping and I did some moves, some choreography with the Turtles. It was a blast and should look good when it's edited and on screen. The song I did was called "Ninja Rap." The idea was dreamed up by the screenwriter, Todd Langdon. Earthquake and I collaborated with him and wrote the music, lyrics and the hook for "Ninja Rap." Not only do I sing it in the movie, it will also be on the soundtrack of the album. That should come out around the same time the movie does, end of March.

I didn't just get up once and do my rap and leave. As I learned in movie making, everything has to be reshot and reshot, seemed like 85 times. So just like everyone else, I had to be ready any time they called to keep on redoing my part. It was a week of "rehearse, go back to the hotel, come back, rehearse some more, leave and then come back again and shoot." So this is the glamor of showbiz! But I didn't see anyone complaining, and I didn't either. The big pay-off's gonna come when I see myself up there on the big screen. Can't wait for it!

During the week we were in Wilmington, I made

the best of it. Me, John Bush, Earthquake and the other people in our group stayed at the Ramada Inn there and spent most of our off time at a restaurant called Hooters where they had the best buffalo wings. They were delicious. We went there pretty much every single day.

There's no question about the best part of the whole Turtles thing. *That* came on my 23rd birthday, October 31, Halloween. My record company gave me a surprise party that I will never forget, not in my whole entire life. They kept it a good secret, and so did Tommy.

There I was dressed up as a sniper, my usual Halloween costume, when they asked me to come into the commissary—that's a movie word for cafeteria. I get there and man, *everyone* is there! The president of my record company, executives from the company, all the Turtle people and Tommy had flown in my entire family, my mother, my brother and his wife, my sister, Byron, everyone. It was slammin'! They brought this huge birthday cake with a picture of my face etched into (what else?) the icing, and they presented me with my first gold and platinum record awards. The record had just gone Number One and at that moment, I was livin' the biggest thrill of my life.

I got presents from everyone. That was when SBK Records gave me the gold Number One pendant. My family gave me some road racing video games they knew I wanted, I got Miami sports t-shirts and the Turtle producer gave me a director's chair with my name and the name of the movie on it. There was food and music and everyone was dancing, forming a conga line, singing. It was the best party I was ever at. And it was my most unforgettable birthday, I'll tell you that. Whenever I think of making the Turtle movie, I'll think about that party.

Teenage Mutant Ninja Turtles II: The Secret Of The Green Ooze hasn't even come out, but we've already had a whole bunch of other movie offers. They wanted me to be in the latest *Nightmare On Elm Street* sequel—and I would have wanted to—but I didn't have room in my schedule to take time off for it.

We've been offered all kinds of films by the biggest movie companies in the business. We've turned them all down—so far, anyway. What we know for sure is that Vanilla Ice will *not* be doing a rap movie and Vanilla Ice will not be doing a "buddy" movie, where they'd team me up with another male star, like Nick Nolte and Eddie Murphy in *48 Hours*. I *would* like to be teamed up with a female, yeah, I could get into *that* easily. But so far, nothing's come our way that we've liked well enough to commit to. Only thing I can tell you for sure is, *yes* I will be doing full blown major movies, that is definitely in the scheme of things.

One thing I've done a lot of and plan to continue with is being on TV. I don't mean *acting* on TV, but I've made a lot of appearances and I plan to keep up with that. I was on *Into The Night* with Rick Dees, *Friday Night Videos* and *Saturday Morning Videos*, a whole week of *MTV's Hot Seat* where I got to play videos. I performed on *Saturday Night Live*, *The American Music Awards* and the biggest thrill, the *MTV Tailgate Party* for the Superbowl.

LIVE ICE

The Hammer tour was sort of like a warm-up for me. I learned, I trained—and now it's time for the *To The Extreme* tour. It's called that not just because of the album, but because that's exactly what it is. I'm headlining and if you haven't seen it yet, you're in for it, big time. Not to ruin the surprise, but I'm lowered onto the stage in a giant ice cube that was designed especially for this tour. We got whole new routines, new posse members, new versions of my songs, new songs!

I am going *all over* with this tour, not just all over the U.S., but Europe, Japan, Australia, there's talk—now I've learned enough to say it's just *talk*, nothing definite yet—that I could be the first rap artist to perform in China! That would be unbelievable—too much! They say that music is the universal language: If rap can have a hand in bringing people together, I want to be there, front and center.

I'm proud to announce that I'm doing a live album, the first ever live rap album—it's gonna be called *Ice Capades* and it is gonna be slammin'! It will be recorded live from the tour, so what I sing onstage is what you're gonna get. That's the album that will finally have "Satisfaction" on it, because the special rap version that I did with my remixer, Gail "Sky" King is what I'm going to sing in concert. It's also going to have four new cuts, some really dope remixes of stuff that Gail's done, an "Ice Ice Baby/Play That Funky Music" medley and a new version of "I Love You," with a group called Riff doing background vocals. They're coming out with me on tour and they're really good.

Along with the live album, we're going to release more singles from *To The Extreme*, probably "Stop That Train" will be a single and "I Love You," which is Charles Koppelman's favorite. Naturally, the soundtrack to the Turtle movie will be happening, so "Ninja Rap" should be out at the same time. Ice is gonna flood the airwaves, kick it hard in 1991!

I'm also planning on more studio albums, and they

will be rap albums. People want me to sing and I *can* sing, but my heart's in rap and that's where it's going to stay. For me, the main focus of my career will stay in rap.

IN STORE ICE

We've also been approached by big companies for endorsements, soda companies, sneaker companies, a video game company. We probably *will* be making announcements about that soon, but as I'm writing this we haven't made any definite deals yet, and I learned the hard way not to jump the gun! But just to let you know—I will be signing with some of these companies and making commercials for them. So you can watch for that.

We'll also be merchandising Ice souvenirs, stuff like t-shirts, posters, baseball caps maybe. What will be fun for me is that I'm getting to design the Vanilla Ice logo on a lot of it. I do have an artistic side and that will be definitely coming at ya' when we get the merchandising aspect in gear.

We've got the fan club going and I just recorded a ton of messages for the Vanilla Ice 900 phone line. It'll be the place to hear me telling you about myself, and about the latest Ice news.

PERSONAL DREAMS

I got some plans and dreams for myself that I hope to get to soon. I'm looking for a new house for myself in the Miami area. I'd like it to overlook the ocean so I could jet ski right up to it. I'd like a swimming pool, a hot tub, a whole bunch of bedrooms so when my friends come over, they can stay. That would be cool.

I dream of winning an *American Music Award*—I got nominated but didn't win yet—and at least one Grammy Award, in the rap categories.

More important than that stuff, though, I'd like to use my celebrity to do more charity work. I have done some: I did a free concert for abused children in San Diego, I've done appearances for homeless people. I'd like to campaign for peace, I even have a sticker out that says "Peace In The Streets." If I can be a force for good in this country, that would be *really* slammin'!

I guess on a personal level, my biggest dream is to be able to share everything I've been given, with my family, my friends and my fans. They've given me so much. All that's happened to me is like winning the lottery, it's God's blessing. I know I lucked out. If I can do good with it, and give something back, I'll feel like I deserve it, like I've earned it.

I'd like to make my mark on the world as an entertainer. Entertaining, feeding people's souls through my music, is what it's all about. I love it. I live for it. Vanilla Ice is here to stay. Yep, yep!!